Chat Rooms in Wonderland

Wayne McDonald

PublishAmerica
Baltimore

First printing

At the specific preference of the author, PublishAmerica allowed this work to remain exactly as the author intended, verbatim, without editorial input.

ISBN: 1-4137-8994-3
PUBLISHED BY PUBLISHAMERICA, LLLP
www.publishamerica.com
Baltimore

Printed in the United States of America

Table of Contents

1. How the Internet (Supposedly) Works 5

2. Chat Rooms in Wonderland 17

3. Chat Room Encounter Sparks International Incident 38

4. The Chat Room Dictionary 41

5. Politics in Wonderland (It's a Conspiracy!) 54

6. A Political Dictionary for Our Time 72

7. Political Correctness in Wonderland 90

8. Religion in Wonderland 100

9. How to Start Your Own Religion: A Guide for Potential Messiahs and Those that Just Want to Screw the IRS 123

10. Book Review: *The Psychology of Cyberspace* 145

11. Sex in Wonderland 151

12. Friends: In All the Right Places 162

1.

How the Internet (Supposedly) Works

If you own a personal computer there is a greater than 99% chance that you have engaged in a practice commonly called "web surfing", in which a person simply enters a subject into the search box and then follows the links that the search engine returns to the browser.

OK, I hear you. "What's a browser?" "What's a search engine?" "I thought a net was something you took with you when you went fishing, not surfing." For those that are unfamiliar with these terms I will attempt to provide a simple explanation.

Someone once referred to the Internet as "the great state where democracy rules." Undoubtedly, whoever said that had never spent much time on line. As the great cynic H. L. Mencken once observed, "Democracy is the act of running the circus from the monkey cage." If the "Sage of Baltimore" were alive today I'm certain that he would refer to the Internet as the act of running the circus from the clown tent.

The Internet can trace its lineage back to the year 1962 when J.C.R. Linklider of the Massachusetts Institute of Technology (MIT) proposed the novel idea of a global network of computers. Shortly thereafter, and after being derided as a crackpot, Linklider moved over to the Defense Advanced Research Projects Agency (DARPA) and began building what we now know as the Internet (at this stage of its evolution the Internet was known as "DARPAnet"). For those of you not familiar with the history and philosophy of DARPA, allow me to explain why this agency is still influencing Internet culture to this very day.

DARPA was formed as a result of a knee-jerk response to the 1957 launch of Sputnik 1 by the then still-united Soviet Union and is an example of an "umbrella" organization. For those who have not yet had the pleasure of dealing with an "umbrella" organization, these creations serve no useful purpose other that to gather all the anarchists into one area where they can ignore each other until a situation arises that makes it more advantageous to gang up on a third party. Umbrella organizations also function in the same way as a conventional umbrella in that both offer a small degree of shelter while the rest of the universe goes out of its way to make your life a miserable Hell.

A few years later (1965, to be semi-exact) Lawrence Roberts of MIT linked a computer in Massachusetts with a computer in California via a standard long-distance telephone call and found that, although it did work, it was unable to handle the large amounts of data required for the two computers to talk to each other. It is suspected (but never documented as true) that Roberts was also the first to say "Dial-up connections suck royally."

By 1969 DARPAnet was still used to connect universities and various military and/or political agencies but, according to Internet historian Walter Howe, this year saw two events that are still applicable today.

Howe reports that:

> Charley Kline of UCLA sent the first packets [of data] via ARPAnet (DARPAnet minus the "D") when he attempted to connect to Stanford Research Institute on October 29, 1969. The system crashed when he reached the "G" in "LOGIN."

This event demonstrates that, although technology has made substantial progress, the probability of a "crash" is still directly proportional to the priority attached to the task.

The second event serves to demonstrate the degree of ignorance in politicians when matters of science are involved.

> Senator Ted Kennedy (D-MA) heard…that the pioneering Massachusetts company BBN had won the ARPAnet contract for an "interface message processor (IMP)," he sent a congratulatory telegram to BBN for their ecumenical spirit in winning the *interfaith* message processor" contract.

ARPAnet grew slowly over the next twenty years as new technologies developed and more universities and research centers joined the network, but the year 1989 marks what many see as the pivotal event in Internet history when Tim Berners-Lee developed something called HTML

HTML stands for the HyperText Markup Language and this is the language that allows the web to work. Or as well as it can work, given the caliber of people using it. Berners-Lee was working for an outfit called CERN, an experimental physics laboratory in Europe that was only slightly less chaotic than DARPA. Berners-Lee saw the advantages of having a common communications format instead of the Babel of languages that were in use at the time. Over time he, and several others, managed to develop a language that organized documents into a formal structure that could include images, text and most importantly, links that allowed the viewer to jump from one part of the document to another part of the same document or even to an entirely different document.

Now HTML, in and of itself, is about as useless as a computer without a power source. The next piece of the puzzle was the creation of the browser and something called the hypertext transfer protocol, or "http." And to get all this data moving around came the advent of machines called routers and servers.

Before we go any further a little "thought experiment" will help to put all this geek-speak into a more understandable format.

Imagine you are in a large house (called www) with twenty rooms, each room containing several filing cabinets with unique files. There are people who roam the halls of this house carrying requests for files to be found and delivering those files to whoever asked for them once they are located. Now imagine that you yell out:

http://www.playboy.com/issues/1995/nancysinatra.htm

One of the people in the hall hears you and then repeats what you said until one of the rooms yells back that they have found that particular item and then tosses it out of the room into the hallway, where it is subsequently tossed from person to person until it lands at your feet.

You, as the one making the request, are using what is called a *browser*. A browser is the thing that lives on your computer that allows you to search the Internet (the www part of your request) for specific information. It does this by using the "http://" thing which, as we learned previously, stands for hypertext transfer protocol. So what you actually said was:

> Using the hypertext transfer protocol, go onto the World Wide Web and find the computer that runs playboy.com. When you find it, ask it for the 1995 issue that had the pictures of the hot babe who wasn't at her father's bedside when he died because she was at home watching "Friends." When you get it, bring it back here to me.

The people in the hall were the *routers*. Routers are the hardware things you never see that take requests and (surprise! surprise!) route them to the proper *servers*, which actually contain whatever it is you are looking for. Servers are also hardware things that you never notice unless they stop doing what they supposed to do, which is to "serve up" the files you requested. When the servers stop working all Hell breaks loose. If the server is not working, due to updating or some other scheduled operation such as routine maintenance, it is said to be "down." Under any other circumstances it is said to have "crashed." Try to think of it like this: Down is much better than crashed when it comes to servers in the same way that "down for maintenance" is better for a Boeing 767 than "crashed into the hanger" would be.

Now, as I said, once they have your pictures for you, the router reverses the process, tracks you down and says to your browser:

Here's ya nude pictures, ya pervert, you're on your own now.

The routers then ignore you until you ask them for something else. Your browser takes all the data you requested and assembles it into readable form for you to enjoy to your heart's, or some other part of your anatomy's content.

Browsers, also known as *web browsers*, are the actual things that make it all possible and come in three flavors:

1. Microsoft Internet Explorer (MSIE)

2. Netscape Navigator (Nutscrape)

3. everyone else (Opera, Firefox, et al)

in that order. In actuality, there is very little difference between any of the available web browsers and it is generally a matter of individual preference that determines which browser to use. But regardless of which browser is being used, you still need some form of access to the Internet. This involves using either an *Internet Service Provider* (ISP) or an *Information Service Gateway*.

ISPs come in many shapes and sizes, from the local "mom and pop" shops that will even go so far as send someone over to your home or office to help you with a problem, to the five hundred-pound gorillas of the industry such as AT&T, Comcast, or NetZero. Given a choice (which most users don't have), using a small local provider rather than one of the large nationwide outfits is generally better because the vast majority of local ISPs actually care about their customers. The nationwide outfits care about their subscribers just long enough to get their money.

If you are comfortable using the Internet or have access to a schoolchild that has learned about computers either at school or while surfing for pornography at the public library, then an ISP is your best bet. Otherwise, you're going to be better off with what is known as an Information Service Gateway. Examples of Gateways are CompuServe or its parent, the company that owns everything that isn't already owned by Microsoft, *America Online* (AOL). Gateways should be avoided, if you possibly can, for several reasons.

The number one reason to avoid using an Information Service Gateway is cost: AOL, on average, is about twice as expensive on a monthly basis as anyone else. And, in some areas you can only get what is known as per-hour billing, which means that you pay for each hour that you spend logged into the company's servers.

Another reason not to use an Information Service Gateway is that they tend to bombard you with e-mails, pop-up ads, or other such distractions trying to unload a product that no one wants or a service that no one needs. The larger Gateways generate a pile of money for themselves with advertising revenue while, at the same time, driving their subscribers nuts.

Since browsers are actually computer programs, they come in

different versions. The version number of a browser can tell you a lot about what level of functionality you can expect and how often the browser will crash, lock up, misdirect your search requests or do any number of other things to make your life a living Hell. Version numbers are generally expressed in "dot notation" such as:

Internet Explorer 6.0.x.x

where the number to the left of the decimal point indicates a major revision or upgrade in functionality (the version number) and the numbers to the right indicate minor revisions (read "bug fixes") that are supposed to represent fine tuning of the browser to "enhance the user experience."

What this means to you, the user, is that the further to the right of the decimal point the number is, the more minor the change in the browser's actual computer code. In reality, what this actually means is that the browser's designers have found a way to make sure that anything that wasn't specifically written for display with that particular browser will not work as intended. This is sometimes a good thing, such as Internet Explorer's inability to display the annoying "blinking" text that Netscape Navigator used to torment early web surfers. Of course, Navigator was unable to display the equally annoying "scrolling marquee" that was only visible to users of Internet Explorer.

It may surprise you to know that, despite using MSIE as its core browser technology, AOL happens to own Netscape lock, devalued stock, and barrel full of monkeys. The fact that AOL doesn't use Netscape as its browser interface is seen by some (those who work for Microsoft) as proof that Microsoft has a superior product. AOL says the actual fact is that Netscape is rapidly gaining on Microsoft and will overtake it soon and AOL wants to be ready when it does. Industry experts predict this will happen around the middle of Jimmy Carter's second term. A small number of other users have said "a pox on both your houses" and will use anything *but* either one of them.

This may seem a little confusing at first, but the history of browsers is actually one of the few interesting things about the whole of what is known as the "Internet Phenomenon."

The "dot com era" is considered to have begun in May of the year 1995 when a company called Netscape "went public." This means that its stock began to be traded on the big stock exchanges and also produced the first wave of instant multi-millionaires. Netscape 1.0 was the first commercially produced web browser and its introduction marked the official arrival of the personal computer, or "PC," as a practical appliance in the home. It was now possible to tap into the mass of knowledge known as "the Internet" without a degree in computer science or having to house a large mainframe computer in the garage or a spare bedroom.

By being the first to introduce a workable browser, Netscape was raking in the cash faster than a topless bar in Daytona Beach during spring break. This caught the attention of a company called Microsoft, which had a virtual monopoly on the one thing that is the most critical component of any computer: the operating system.

Without an operating system, a computer is a collection of components that just sits on your desk, table or wherever and does nothing but attract dust or coffee spills. The operating system is what actually tells all those components what to do and makes them into a functioning computer. Microsoft Corporation, thanks to its visionary founder Bill Gates, provided the operating system for about ninety-five per cent of the computer market in the world, including the systems that run most of the big ISP servers. But Gates and Microsoft, in a rare case of being caught off guard, had drastically underestimated the growth of the home computer market and the popularity of the Internet, and thus originally had no browser available to compete with Netscape's product. And if there is one thing that Microsoft cannot tolerate it is being less than "number one" at anything.

Microsoft then saw a way to totally shut Netscape out of the browser business. Since practically every computer this side of the

Romulan Neutral Zone was sold with Microsoft's Windows operating system already installed, why not include a web browser as part of the package? Who would pay extra for a web browser if one were already installed on the system? Particularly if the installed browser was an integral part of the basic operating system and COULD NOT BE REMOVED, even if the owner of the computer wanted to get rid of it?

The buying public got the message and thanks to Microsoft's "bundling" its browser, Internet Explorer, with the Windows operating system, Netscape was suddenly in the position of trying to sell a product that Microsoft was throwing in for free. Since its browser was the only product that Netscape had, its revenues dried up faster that mud puddle in Yuma, Arizona. Since this is the good old United States of America, you can imagine what happened next.

Netscape cried "Foul," a cry that was soon taken up by the United States Department of Justice in the form of an antitrust and monopolistic trade practices lawsuit pitting Netscape, the Clinton Justice Department, and a horde of state attorneys-general against the evil Microsoft Corporation. The "browser war" was headed for court.

After a few years of depositions, counter-claims, press releases, news conferences and other such wastes of time, Microsoft was bullied into accepting a "settlement" that would have resulted in the company being split apart and gutted as "punishment" for such "illegal" activities as introducing a competing browser. And since this was still the good old United States of America, Microsoft promptly appealed the "settlement" to the next judicial level.

The Appeals Court threw out the settlement on the basis that it was basically motivated by the 1960s-era philosophy of the incumbent Clinton administration, which believed that any corporation as successful as Microsoft had to have attained such success by "immoral" or "illegal" tactics because wealth itself was a sign that such success must have been acquired at the expense of a "victim." The public echoed the sentiments of the court by voting out of office as many members of the Clinton administration as possible.

It was noted by many members of the computer industry that Apple Computers was not a participant in this legal circus, although at one time Apple was "the" desktop computer manufacturer. Most theorized that Apple had no desire to make a public record of its own follies, which could serve as a model for how NOT to survive in the (then) rapidly expanding home computer industry.

If the advantage, in any industry, lies with being the first to market a product, Apple should have had the home computer business sewn up from day one. In the early 1980s, they practically invented the home computer market with the first computer that was designed for, well, the home. The first Apple computer signaled the early days of the "computer industry," which until then had meant making very large machines that only the likes of General Motors or the Defense Department could afford. Not only did Apple make the computer hardware, it also made the operating system. And that was what eventually forced Apple out of the catbird seat.

Apple, since it owned the only operating system available at the time, was in a position to rake in billions of dollars by licensing its technology to other developers and manufacturers who would then pay Apple a royalty fee for the privilege of using its operating system. But Apple would not license its technology, which meant that there was no incentive for others to develop applications such as word processors, spread sheets, file management systems or other such programs that the business (and eventually the home) users were crying for.

Then along came a small company called Microsoft, which capitalized on Apple's intransigent position and the rest, as they say, is history.

Despite all this legal wrangling over who got to provide the user with them, browsers would be pretty bland things if not for something called a *search engine*. Search engines are the special programs that take the term or item you wish to locate on the Internet and return a set of hits, lists of web sites that seem to match your request. This is not always the case, unfortunately.

For example, suppose you enter the word "CATS!" in your browser's search window and tell the browser to ask the search engine for sites that match that request. Depending on the search engine being used you will get hits on sites that:

1) Are devoted to the common house pet

2) Are devoted to the larger cousins of the above

3) Are about the Broadway show

4) have things like "I play with my pussy a lot! Want to watch me?"

An even more interesting thing happens when you use AOL as your ISP. Suppose you enter the term "man-portable nuclear bombs", what do you think you get back? Well, of course you get back web sites that match your search request but you also get back a bunch of AOL-generated advertising links such as:

Read more about man-portable nuclear bombs at Britannica.com

Buy books about man-portable nuclear bombs at Barnes and Noble.com

Visit kids-only sites that feature man-portable nuclear bombs

Sell your extra man-portable nuclear bombs on e-bay.com

Order more man-portable nuclear bombs from Lands End online

AOL is, of course, not the only outfit to torment its subscribers with such nonsense. But it is definitely the most blatant.

The more technically oriented of you (or the purely masochistic)

might ask, "With all these different companies doing their own thing, how does anyone know what will or what won't work on the Internet?" Believe it or not, there is actually a group that has the thankless task of deciding what everyone should do to insure that the whole thing works as advertised. This group of people is a loose confederation of industry representatives (read "another umbrella organization") that argue among themselves until everyone decides that they will never agree on anything and a compromise emerges. This is the role of the World Wide Web Consortium, or as it is more commonly known, the W3C.

The W3C, like the United Nations, has absolutely no power to enforce its decisions, which are known as "recommendations." This means that they study a proposal for several years, consulting among themselves while they issue a series of documents known as "proposed recommendations", "working drafts", "requests for comments" or "requests for more E-Z Widers" prior to publishing the final standard that everyone is supposed to follow.

In actuality this document is (of course) not worth the cyber-paper it's printed on, but it does serve a very useful purpose in that everyone now knows what to ignore in the next release of their particular products. This is the reason why something that is a work of art when viewed with MSIE resembles the handiwork of a dyslexic four-year-old when viewed with anything else.

Now that you are armed with the minimum amount of knowledge required to understand how the Internet actually works, feel free to join the rest of us as we try to avoid becoming road kill along the side of the information superhighway.

2.

Chat Rooms in Wonderland

One of my favorite pastimes is to observe, from a safe distance, the follies of society. And in my opinion, by whatever process we humans became the dominate species on this planet, we did so while developing as many antisocial and self-destructive habits as possible.

To confirm the above opinion, I recently began using the Yahoo chat rooms again. You will notice I use the word "again", since I did chat quite a lot a few years ago. I stopped when I noticed that the World Wide Web, originally designed as a tool to allow communication between research facilities and government officials in the event of global thermonuclear war, had degenerated into something less than electronic anarchy.

Of course, working for a year in Saudi Arabia was also a factor in that protracted silence. Not only does the Saudi government censor incoming mail but it also blocks practically all chat rooms and e-mail (unless, of course, you use them to communicate with your friends in Hezbollah or Al-Quaeda).

For those of you not familiar with the unique form of self-abuse known as the chat room, allow me to provide a short description.

A chat room was originally a place hosted by companies such as Yahoo, AOL, or the Microsoft Network where you could type messages to friends or meet people from almost anywhere on the planet. There were different classes of rooms depending on your age, your interests, sexual orientation or practically any combination of things you could imagine. Hell, you could even join a room with the name "Nuke the Homeless Gay Baby Whales for Jesus" if you wanted to. But it didn't stay that way for long.

As my hero and role model H.L. Mencken so correctly stated: "The only problem with communism is the communists, just as the only problem with Christianity is the Christians." I would like to amend that statement to include "and the only problem with chat rooms is the chatter." Allow me explain what led me to this conclusion.

Truth Is the First Casualty of War (and Chat Rooms)

Chat rooms are an example of how the created can turn around and corrupt the creators. In the case of chat rooms it works by becoming both a mirror image of human society and an extension of it, with the exception that in chat rooms there is no peer pressure to maintain anything even close to the mask of civility.

The term "chat room" is an oxymoron, somewhere between "honorable politician" and "army intelligence" on the self-contradictory scale. Most chat rooms are basically private clubs where people with similar high opinions of themselves come to fight their own feelings of insecurity by acting out fantasies of their own self-importance. They do this by making anyone outside their own little circle into a second-class citizen by either forcing the "intruder" to beg to be acknowledged or by subjecting them to ridicule by the "elect of the chat Gods."

If this serves some need of society I have yet to understand what it might be, unless it cuts down on the number of people who walk into fast food restaurants with automatic weapons and kill 20 people because the shooter didn't have a date for the prom.

The chat room "nation" has even created its own language that allows its citizens to communicate with each other without being understood by the rest of the civilized world. A few of these words, phrases or abbreviations you will encounter regularly are:

A/S/L: an acronym that dates from the earliest days of chat rooms and originally was used to ask the question "Age? Sex? Location?" of another chatter. It is currently used to indicate that the person using this statement is an idiot/loser/new chat room user, as anyone else would know that this statement is "passé" among the upper crust of chat room citizens.

BBW: Big Bodied Woman, a polite way of saying "fat bitch." It usually indicates the presence of a Bloated Beached Whale.

Boot, the: being disconnected from a chat program for reasons that are never quite clear or even the same.

BRB: Be Right Back. *Bath Room Break* if the chatter has been boozing it up, a fairly common event when in chat rooms.

Cheeta: a chat program that allows a chatter to be obnoxious in more than one chat room simultaneously.

Hai: A word of both uncertain origin and definition, although the current trend is to favor Sanskrit for the former and "I wish to be sodomized by the syphilitic goat" for the latter.

ICQ: a chat program that allows the users to manage all their other chat programs, e-mail accounts, passwords etc. and is thus far too sophisticated to be used by the average chatter since the instructions for its use do not include a box of crayons.

IM: Instant Message; a way for two chatters to communicate in private, thus denying the rest of the chat universe the chance to learn what the two parties have been up to. It is a favorite toll of people with no concept of politeness to pester other users with messages that invariably begin with "A/S/L."

LMAO: Laughing My Ass Off, a response to the rare event of someone saying an unusually funny remark but commonly used when another chatter has made an unusually prominent fool of themselves.

LOL: Laughing Out Loud, a milder response than "LMAO." In some instances it may be defined to mean "Loser, Oh Loser."

PM: Private Message, a synonym for IM and abused with the same frequency.

Voice: A tool of Satan that allows the illiterate to be just as obnoxious as any other chatter.

Although, to my knowledge, there has never been a psychosocial study that profiles the average or typical chatter I would not hesitate to wager that it would look something like this:

> The typical chatter is someone who is usually outside what could be considered the social mainstream, be it for reasons of physical appearance or lack of social relational skills. Most chatters would be considered unattractive in their primary social units, which has led them to adopt various self-defense mechanisms including self-aggrandizement, overstatement of physical attributes or social class, or some other combination of self-promotional behavior to compensate for their actual or perceived shortcomings.

For those that do not recognize politically correct gibberish when you see it, allow me to restate the previous paragraph.

> Most chatters are so ugly that they could start a general panic in the monkey exhibit at the San Diego Zoo and are about three neurons away from doing a Son of Sam routine. Since they have finally figured out that they don't qualify as shark bait, they have deluded themselves into thinking that they have fooled everyone else in chat into thinking that they are the apple of Mother Nature's eye.

And it doesn't seem to change. It's always the same people in the same chat room at the same time, and usually feeding each other's slightly unbalanced impression of themselves. I don't mean to imply that some chatters are pathologic liars, but consider the following observation.

I have yet to visit a chat room and see three consecutive true statements in the course of normal conversation. In fact, I have yet to see three consecutive complete sentences of any degree of veracity.

There are some exceptions to this that are most likely explained by statistical aberrancy. The most common situation arises when someone is so offensive, stupid, ignorant, annoying or ill-mannered (in other words, another typical chatter) that this person provokes at least three people say "You're an asshole." This may be either a rare example of a true statement in a chat room or the ultimate instance of being called ugly by a pond full of frogs.

I have also noticed that chat rooms have the mysterious effect of causing beneficial changes in physical appearance. It is indeed rare to find any female chatter who has not been transformed from someone who could induce nausea at a coroner's convention into the reincarnation of the Queen of Sheba.

Males are also subject to this unexplained metamorphosis, with enlargement of the penis being the most common finding. In fact, this enlargement and elongation is so remarkable as to prompt the beneficiary to proudly add the fact to his screen name and then attempt to mate with as many of these neo-Aphrodites as possible. Which brings us to the topic of cyber-sex.

There is a pseudo-law of science called the "Law of Unintended Consequences," which states:

> No matter the intent of the original idea, someone will find a way to totally screw up even the best of intentions.

I know of no better example of this than the practitioners of what is commonly described as cyber-ex.

In the same way that primitive man first observed that the sharpened stick that he used to protect himself from saber-toothed tigers was much more effective when applied to the backs of his unsuspecting cave-mates, cybersex has evolved as a way for people who would normally be resigned to a lifetime of enforced celibacy to hijack a simple biologic process and distort it beyond recognition. Fortunately, there has been no conclusive evidence of the existence of a cybergene pool to be contaminated by these reality refugees.

For the uninitiated or the totally ignorant, cybersex is the process of that allows two or more people (gender is not a factor) to live out delusional fantasies of their sexual prowess without fear of physically encountering each other, thus avoiding the discovery of another life form further down the evolutionary tree than themselves.

Cybersex is generally initiated after a conversation such as:

He: WOW! Washing my Mercedes makes me really hot for some sexy babe!

She: I know! I feel the same way when I go to Maui for my *Sports Illustrated* photo session!

Another: Hai!! a/s/l please

Allow me to translate the above cyber-babble into plain English.

He: My pickup truck needs an oil change, but my wife drove it to the tattoo parlor.

She: If I could get down to size 24, I could fit through the door at the new K-Mart in Spartanburg.

Another: i am from obscuristan. you yes will talk dirty on me

Having made contact with a potential breeding partner they will begin a verbal courtship ritual in which they explore the others suitability as a temporary mate. When both are satisfied that that their high standards have been met, they disappear into the traditional breeding grounds known as "the loft." They will then copulate with such force and stamina that motion detection monitors in every nuclear power plant from Bangor, Maine to Las Vegas, Nevada will think that the wooly mammoths have returned and mere mortals will cringe in fear lest they be reduced to ashes by this supernova of newly discovered love as it flames through the skies of cyberspace.

But sadly, Eros is as fickle in cyberspace as on Mount Olympus and all true love is again lost. Some will return to reality to avoid detection by their spouses, their parents will unplug the modem, or the sheep will see an opening and make a break for it. Some will never find their one true love. And some, at the height of multi-orgasmic joy, will accidentally hit the "DELETE" button. This will have the tragic effect of removing any and all physical enhancements acquired in the chat rooms, thus returning the sword to the stone, the inflatable doll to the closet, and the batteries to the flashlight.

Screen Names and Other Works of Fiction

As noted previously, truth is rarer in chat rooms than it is in the halls of Congress and all the singles bars of Los Angeles County combined. Most chatters think that by choosing a screen name that conveys the impression of physical attractiveness that either one of two things will happen. The first (and most likely to occur) is that someone will actually be dumb enough to believe that the user is the next Pamela Anderson Lee. The other (and much less likely to happen) is that by adopting a sensual name some magic transformation will occur and the chatter will be converted from the ear, or some other part of the sow, into a silky siren. It has been conclusively proven that Oral Roberts, Reverend Ike and Benny Hinn combined don't carry enough clout with the Almighty to pull off that big a miracle.

I really can't speak for the rest of the chat room users but I like to use a screen name that reflects something that I identify with, such as literature or philosophy. I sometimes get the impression that many chatters have other things on what is left of their minds besides honesty and virtue. But since that is obvious to anyone who has spent more than five minutes in a chat room, let's take a look at some screen names.

I personally use the name "Audens_tears", which I adopted in honor of the late poet W. H. Auden. The "tears" portion comes from the fact that chat rooms can bore me to tears in less time than it takes to explain what the name means to the average semi-literate chatter. I have other names that I use, of course, but they are reserved for special occasions, like playing mind-games with the idiots who think that people are actually stupid enough to buy the line of male bovine excrement that they use when trying to impress others that are in the same situation as themselves: being so far down the social ladder they have nothing to look forward to other than another a day in a chat room.

Some chat names are deliberately chosen to convey something about the personality of the chatter, but since most chatters are woefully lacking in the personality department we can dismiss these instances as merely coincidences. However, some names are pure masterpieces.

The one name that I have seen that causes more double takes among the male members of the Yahoid species is the classic "womanwithballs." This stroke of pure genius has caused more confusion and sent more males into a castration-complex panic than a drunken Rabbi at a circumcision seminar. Nothing gets "bubba_from_the_truckstop" or "hot_12_inches_4_u" into a state of gender confusion quicker than the idea that some woman would not find them to be their dream come true, much less confuse them with a metaphorical statement. The concepts of metaphor and hyperbole are totally wasted on a population that confuses Marvel Comics with English literature.

And Walter Mitty is still alive and well in Yahoo. If even half of the names I have seen are even remotely close to describing the actual profession of the users, Yahoo is the safest place in the universe. They have dozens of "texas_ranger"s, "bounty_hunter"s, and even a few "star ship_trooper"s among the chatters. This is on top of all the "navy_seal"s, "green_beret"s, "airborne_ranger"s, "retired_marine"s and various other military or para-military types wandering around the chat rooms in such numbers that the United States could wipe out Iran and the rest of the "Axis of Evil" with Yahoo chat room users alone!

If the Economy Is So Bad, Where Do All Those Ads Come From?

The myth of the "dot com" collapse is finally shattered by the seemingly endless number of unsolicited e-mails, drive-bys, bots, and other minions of Satan that torment the chat room user. These abominations are generally of the form:

Do_you_like_to_have_sex?
Meet_me_at_http://www.dumbyahoopeckerwood/horny/andhopeless.asp

and, once luring the unsuspecting or dim-witted chatter into their realm, ensnare him forever in a netherworld of eternally opening windows that promote every vice known to the animal kingdom.

But there is one example of this type of ad that is so patently stupid that it makes me wonder if the third grade dropout who wrote it ever stopped to think if anyone was dumb enough to respond.

Do you want to meet someone like you?
Visit Lisa @ http:www.find_my_soulmate.com

"Hell Yes! I've been looking for another middle aged, bald headed, chain-smoking, beer guzzling asshole for years! Sign me up now!"

It may purely coincidental, but these ads seemed to explode into Yahoo chat shortly after Yahoo acquired GeoCities.com. If cyberspace is the global community, GeoCities.com was its red light district. It was, at the time it was purchased by Yahoo, the home of every phone sex, get rich quick scheme, and credit card fraud operation on the Internet. But as far as Yahoo was concerned it had one very good point: it had a steady revenue stream. Not wanting to offend any of its new paying customers, Yahoo opened the doors of chat to every scam that existed in that virtual Babylon. The result is that a visit to a chat room is like a walk down 42nd Street at midnight. To be fair to Geocities, as the cost of operating a web site fell to almost nothing most of these operations switched over to self-hosting or something else and left it to Geocities to provide free web pages for Yahoo subscribers.

If these ads are generating an average of one cent in revenue for Yahoo per appearance, Yahoo will soon be bigger than Microsoft. This would not be a good thing in that Yahoo software is less stable than the Italian government. Chat software seems to spend most of its time crashing, freezing, or just plain screwing up. At least Microsoft has periodic bug fixes available, but Yahoo merely repackages the bugs for use in future versions. You know the old saying, "You get what you pay for"? Welcome to Yahoo, sucker!

The opposing camp holds that the economy is indeed in the toilet and that the people named Sherry, Monica, Chelsea or some other snotty London suburb who constantly ask inane questions about kissing or sex are actually a new species of cyber-children produced by those engaging in unsafe cybersex.

Not all these annoying ads are related to sex. There is a growing tendency for those with some type of social, political, or religious agenda that must be brought to your immediate attention to utilize this same technology, which is so abrasive as to cause some users to flee to the nearest monastery and take vows of celibacy rather than see one more ad for Jeanie's web cam and phone sex club, to harass the chatter with statements such as:

It's_time_for_a_new_generation!
Join_us_at_http://www.Lobotomized FlowerChild.org

Or

Gore_was_cheated!
Read_how_at_http://www.DNC.com/losers/whyme.htm

And of course the ever popular

Jesus is coming soon!!
Get ready at http://www.godispissed/tolduso/asshole.asp

or some other tripe that manages to insult the intelligence of anyone who ever drove past a middle school.

Sadly, these ads fail to receive even a small percentage of the scorn that they merit. If someone ever came up with a program that would send an equally ridiculous reply to these things, I would personally pay royalties to make sure that every chat user in whatever chat program would have it instantly available to respond with messages like

about friggin' time jesus got back to work! tell him to go get all the flower children and teach them how to read and write because gore needs all the help he can get!

I would like to propose an international holiday, which I call "International Fry the Drive-bys and Script bots Day." On this day at a prearranged time, a signal would be given which would cause every computer user in the world to respond to as many of these ads as possible. The resulting overload of their creator's hardware would cause "a catastrophic system-wide infrastructure failure" (it would melt their servers into a slag pile, for those of you not familiar with geek-speak), which would hopefully cause these jerks to think twice about bothering the pimple-faced overweight social rejects who just want to get laid in cyberspace without being made to feel guilty about it.

Voice Chat Is Another Sign That The Apocalypse Is Near

Many years ago (six to be exact) there was no such animal as voice chat. In those dark days a chatter had to be able to read and write, at least on a rudimentary level. Chat was also one hell of a lot more fun back then. I can distinctly remember when it was possible to have intelligent conversations several times in a single day and think nothing of it. But to paraphrase Margaret Mitchell, "those days are gone with the wind." And the wind that blew Yahoo straight into Ya-hell was a mighty gust of hot air called voice chat.

Now don't get me wrong. I don't mean to imply that voice chat is a bad thing. It can always be cited as an example of how even the best of intentions can become so distorted that it becomes unrecognizable, even to its creator. Other, more recognizable, examples of this phenomenon are communism, Christianity, affirmative action, and the Democratic Party.

Voice chat was originally created as a means of allowing the physically challenged to participate in chat rooms. It has since devolved into a tool that the mentally, morally and/or emotionally handicapped use to torment those who can read and write above Sesame Street level. You need only be in voice chat for five minutes before some disembodied voice intones the sacred words of the Divine Brotherhood of Yahoo:

How ya'll doin' tonight? Sure would lak to chat with a purty girl or two!

The voice chatters have also undergone the mysterious transformations that were described earlier. But in addition to becoming gods and goddesses they, just like Balaam's ass, can speak. Please note that I did not say speak intelligently. You are much more likely to hear

> sittin' at my 'puter grinnin' lak a possum eatin' shit

than you are to hear

> I am sitting in my computer room with the facial expression of a nocturnal North American marsupial consuming fecal matter.

The typical voice chatter is so in love with his/her own voice that he/she cannot wait to bless the rest of the world with its melodious airs. Whether the world wants to hear it is of no concern to this particular species of chatter, since they (and their close circle of the chosen ones) are here to preach the gospel according to Yahoo. They have also taken a sacred oath to be as snobbish as possible whenever some unsuspecting soul admits to not using voice, thus incurring their wrath and scorn. Nothing is more disturbing to the voice chatter than the thought that there is someone out there that has not had the privilege of hearing them speak.

Voice has also allowed these same people to inflict their horrible tastes in music upon others. Not being content to merely destroy the English language, the "voice snobs" soon learned that they could also trash the whole of western civilization with music that is so bad that you won't hear it on an all-night AM radio station in Spokane. Now any garage band with a tape recorder can reach the entire world with a cacophony of sounds resembling something of a hybrid of punk rock and the sound track of a National Geographic special. This is, of course, in addition to the usual garbage that somehow passes for music.

And practically no genre of music seems exempt from this form of cyber-broadcasting, although I can't recall having heard either Bach or Wagner in a chat room recently. For some reason, the people who want to be a cyberspace disc jockey play nothing but country music. Bad country music. I believe that the time has come to see a law passed that establishes the death penalty as punishment for the crime of playing "Achy Breaky Heart", or any other form of recorded animal torture commonly known as country music, in a chat room.

There are times, however, that being in a room full of voice chatters is more fun than having Mike Tyson as your probation officer. I am referring, of course, to those times when a technical malfunction occurs which renders voice chat inoperable. If you want to see the chat room version of the Great Panic of 1929, just wait until the voice servers crash and force those who are addicted to voice chat to read and write instead. This usually results in a torrent of gibberish resembling a Jackie Chan movie with Navajo subtitles played in reverse. The products of our superior American public schools are totally lost when forced to use skills that are considered basic anywhere else in the civilized world, with the possible exception of Montana and most of Texas.

When the voice chatters are deprived of their favorite toy they immediately lose the ability to communicate with each other and, for once, are subject to the same ridicule that they are so fond of heaping onto the less-enlightened souls who either do not have or else elect not to use voice as their primary means of chatting. This usually confirms the widely held impressions that the "voicers" have absolutely no sense of humor at all. The voicers will also immediately swear a blood oath to exact revenge on those who have dared to point out that the voice chatters are a conclusive rebuttal to an extrapolation of the room-full-of-monkeys-with-typewriters theory.

This theory, which predates the computer era by at least fifty years, states that a room full of monkeys randomly striking the keys on a typewriter would eventually reproduce the *Encyclopedia Britannica*. However, a room full of voice chatters being forced to type will never be able to produce a complete sentence no matter how much time they are given to accomplish the task.

Peek-A-Boo, I See You!

Shortly after the advent of voice chat some sadist decided that if voice is good, voice with pictures would be even better. Thus was born the most recent imp of the devil that no self-centered chatter should do without, the web cam.

Web cams are small devices that allow the world the distinctive privilege of viewing your exalted personage while listening to your divine voice (or reading your holy words). What I have yet to discover is why anyone that thinks they are so gifted by the chat gods would want the rest of the world to see them as they really are. The fact that they have hidden their actual names and true physical description for so long is indeed remarkable, so why do they blow their own fantasies out of the water with a web cam?

My personal theory is that they have, a la propaganda, told a big enough lie so many times that even they now believe it. The advent of the web cam has killed more chat room romances than the dreaded Yahoo boot. That sultry voice which has seduced the unwary chatter is suddenly realized to be attached to someone who looks like Stone Cold Steve Austin in drag! And there is not enough Viagra in North America to recover from that shock to the hyperactive imagination.

The online voyeur and exhibitionist communities have quickly accepted web cams, as it frees them of the intellectual challenge of having to imagine what the other party looks like while simultaneously maintaining a state of sexual arousal. For the exhibitionist, this means they have a way to offend many more people in the same amount of time as previously required to offend (or arouse) only one. The voyeurs are now spared the stress of having to prowl the unsafe streets at night while evading the local constabulary or meeting someone sicker then themselves.

However I did find one very useful application for this technology. Believe me, there is no greater emotional rush than the one you get after "mooning" some moron that has been bombarding you for half an hour with his gibberish about sex. It's too bad that you can't see the response it generates. The mere thought of some third-world turkey spanking the monkey and suddenly getting a screen full of someone's skinny ass taxes both the imagination's ability to visualize such a scene and the adequacy of the English language to describe it.

It Ain't a Theory, Charlie!

It took Charles Darwin three years on a smelly Royal Navy sailing ship to acquire the data that led to his famous theories of natural selection and evolution from lower, simpler life forms into more advanced species. He could have saved a lot of time by spending a week in a chat room.

If it pleases the court of public opinion, I would like to propose a new social and anthropometrical classification system for use in chat rooms.

Normal: An endangered species whose ultimate fate remains undetermined. Each chat room user is free to apply their own definition to this category.

Neo-lithic Predator: This group has formed primitive social units and mastered fire. It has not developed a written language and its social evolution has arrested at the hunter-gatherer stage. It is estimated that 70% of the adult males in chat fall into this mob.

Ante-deluvian Reptile: A member of this group is unable to maintain internal body temperature, has an underdeveloped cerebral cortex, and has only recently adapted to living on land. A representative of this class will be found in every chat room.

Primordial Plankton: A complete waste of protoplasm. A member of this group is incapable of writing anything other than "hai a/s/l, how are you? You lak the sex with ______ guy who is hot 4 u?"

Comments from the scientific community regarding this proposal are requested but will be ignored if found not to be supportive of the proposed classification schema.

Along these same lines, I have noticed that certain geographic regions seem to have their own distinctive brand of chatters. Citizens of the vast wasteland commonly known as Texas seem to fit best into the Neolithic predator category. They also seem to have enacted a law requiring anyone residing within the borders of that tropical paradise to have:

A screen name that mentions cowboy/girl, rose, Texas, or rodeo

An IQ less than the room number

A pickup truck

An infinite supply of country music

A total lack of personality

Cyber-sex with someone more repulsive than themselves at least once a night

some other combination of social dysfunctions

The Texans tend to congregate into cliques of loosely formed tribes of six or more males and a smaller number of females, with the females compensating for the lack of numerical parity with a larger body surface area.

Texas chatters are in love with themselves to a point of fault. Both sexes are certain they are the standard that all others should emulate. If this was true the world would soon be populated by 225-pound women with the audacity to wear Spandex shorts and cowboy boots in public. And if that visual didn't get your attention can you imagine the type of male that would be chasing this fashion statement all over downtown Odessa on Saturday night? Or what their children would look like? Fortunately these people have elected to confine themselves to a geographic area that most civilized human beings avoid whenever possible.

And if you think that you've had a few strange conversations in your life, log into an Internet chat room some day. This is an example of one of the more literate conversations.

Idiot: a/s/l please
Me: male, now go away
(pause)

Idiot: i am from obscuristan. you will yes speak on me?
Me: no. now get lost!
(another pause)

Idiot: a/s/l please
Me: what part of "shut the f__k up" don't you understand?
(longer pause)

Idiot: i have the big cock and am like big breasts
Me: Glad to hear you raise big chickens. Now get lost, son of a pig and a dog
(another long pause)

Idiot: you will talk dirty for me yes
Me: your daughter works in a Pakistani whorehouse
(pause)

Idiot: son of a bitch
Me: good observation, want to try for two in a row?

And so on and so on until I finally just put the idiot on the "Ignore for Eternity" list.

It is also well-known that, for some reason, the current residents of that part of the United States known as the South, the old South, the Confederacy or some other regional euphemism, have a special affinity for voice chat as well as the unique ability to type with what is commonly known as a "southern drawl." Why anyone would go through the trouble to type in such a manner as to prove that they are masters of mutilating the English language when voice chat relieves them from the intellectual challenge of consulting a dictionary is totally beyond explanation.

I hope that my comments about the average Yahoo users have had the results I intended, which was to show how ridiculous they appear when they take themselves seriously. I am sure that by now, many of them are in the early stages of either a hypertensive crisis or are busily plucking the yard birds to insure that an adequate amount of feathers will be on hand for my well-deserved tar and feathers tuxedo, which will be an upcoming event only if Bubba can steal enough tar from the Highway Department and "sweet_dixie_darlin'" can get the diesel stains out of the bed sheets before the next cross burning and hot dog supper.

But please do not think me as one of the race-baiting xenophobes that seem to be rearing their ugly heads in chat rooms these days. As you can easily see, I hold the vast majority of my fellow Americans in the same low regard.

How I Rate Chat Room Users with Applied Mathematics

As a programmer, I use certain equations to determine how well a given computer program will react to different situations or user errors. I have extended some of these equations in an attempt to create a simple chat room user scoring system.

The evolution of the equation itself is of no concern but it can be summarized as:

LOSER = (i+a) / (tti+bpi2)

Where LOSER is defined as the "Logical Observed Social and Emotional Rating." (i+a) is the sum of the IQ and the age in years divided by the sum of the "tooth/tattoo index' and the square of the 'body part index" The "tti" is obtained by dividing the number of remaining natural teeth by the number of visible tattoos. The "bpi" is determined by squaring the number and size of any body parts mentioned in the screen name.

It will also be noted that although this is still a work in progress, I theorize that the larger the LOSER index, the more likely the subject under evaluation will be an acceptable conversationalist. This may seem counterintuitive on first inspection, but can easily be explained.

This is a chat room! And as Alice discovered in her trip to Wonderland, things are never as they seem.

3.

Chat Room Encounter Creates International Incident

The strained relations between Obscuristan and the United States were taken to near crisis levels after an incident in a Yahoo chat room threatened to destabilize an already tenuous relationship.

Although details remain sketchy due to problems with Yahoo, according to witnesses at the scene of the confrontation the incident began when a certain "patel_bigdik" refused to believe that another chatter known only as "Audens_tears" was not a woman. After stating that he was in fact a dead gay poet, "Audens_tears" attempted to gracefully defuse the situation by activating his web cam to resolve the dispute permanently. "Patel_bigdik" responded that he would "like to see big American breasts have you", prompting "Audens_tears" to question both his adversary's sexual orientation and in which part of the animal kingdom "patel_bigdik's" parents originated.

"Audens_tears" then gracefully invited the entire room, including "patel_bigdik ", to view his web cam as he would indeed show the room "some real hooters." After all had joined, "Audens_tears" shocked the spectators by not revealing his breasts for public display but instead dropping his trousers and "mooning" "patel_bigdik" along with numerous innocent bystanders.

Reaction to the incident was rapidly felt throughout the world. According to unconfirmed reports "patel_bigdik" could only respond with seemed to most eyewitnesses as gibberish but, as none of them understood a word that he was saying, it could well have been that he found himself in the throes of multi-orgasmic joy. One witness at the scene, who gave his name as "aussie_with_an_attitude" stated, "Its about time somebody got the damned rag heads to shut up, cant have a bloody decent spot of chat without them mailing you with their damned monkey-talk and such! I say bugger the lot of them!" Yahoo officials were not immediately available for comment

The American diplomatic community seemed to be caught off-guard by the sudden developments. A State Department official would only confirm that aides to Secretary of State Condoleeza Rice were "monitoring events closely to insure that this does not escalate into some type of cyber-war" with the potential to "seriously destabilize a region already populated by unstable people."

He went on to state "We are skeptical of Obscuristani claims that the incident is a new round of Italian-sponsored state terrorism. If this does give them the excuse they need to engage in regional thermonuclear warfare, we see that this would be self-limiting in nature and of no strategic importance to the long term interests of the United States or any of our NATO allies."

When pressed to explain this abrupt change in US policy, he replied "Who gives a shit if they blow each other from here to the Klingon home world? We might have to train more cab drivers and 7-11 clerks, but so what?"

Others echoed the same sentiments. According to a Time/CNN poll taken within hours of the incident, 97% reported that they agreed with the dramatic response made by "Audens_tears" and said that they would have done the same thing. CNN anchor Wolf Blitzer stated that although the poll seemed to show a ground swell of public support, they were unable to question enough Obscuristani citizens to insure the poll was accurate. Blitzer reported that the only replies received to the e-mail questions posed to citizens of that poverty-stricken but computer-rich country were "talk dirty on my face" and "a/s/l please."

There were also signs of positive support from within the business community as well. A spokesperson for e-bay, the online auction giant, stated that sales of web cams were up by 75% from the previous day with similar reports being received from all the major US retailers. There were unconfirmed reports that Microsoft chairman and CEO Bill Gates was engaged in a bidding war with arch-rival Yahoo.com for rights to use images from the encounter in their respective message and chat programs. An unidentified source close to top Yahoo management said the company was very close to signing a deal that would allow it to use those images as part of their "emotions" package in future releases of their highly popular products, replacing the "sad smiley" with a computer-generated image of "Audens_tears'" anorexic Caucasian buttocks.

4.

The Chat Room Dictionary

@^(*%#@&()^%$!4!

*@prodigy**** (adj.): See *@sbcglobal**** and *Hai*, below

*@sbcglobal****(adj.): a postscript to a screen name that identifies a domestic variety of pest, usually of the wanna-be variety, that is incapable of understanding why no one is impressed with his/her sexual prowess. See *Hai* (below).

A

ACK (?): a term of self-criticism used by a chatter to denote that at least a portion of a previous statement was incorrect. Given the intellectual capacity of a significant number of chatters, it probably evolved due to the fact that "I'm sorry, I entered my last statement incorrectly." would tax their ability to a level that could lead to brain damage, if not already clinically present.

Addy (abbr.): a shortened form of the word "address", used to denote a certain location on the Internet such as a person's e-mail address (e-mail addy) or the URL of a particular web site.

Adult chat room (misnomer): a circle of Hell that went unrecognized by Dante and is populated by every conceivable form of cyber-pervert from exhibitionist to transgendered cross-dressers. The number of chronological adults in adult chat at a given time has never been accurately determined, but is believed to be less that five per cent. If mental adulthood was to be the selected as the criteria for inclusion in this group, the percentage would undoubtedly fall to a considerably lower number.

A/S/L (abbr.): an acronym, which dates from the earliest days of chat rooms and originally was used to ask the question "What is your Age? Sex? Location?" of another chatter. It is currently interpreted as an indication that the person using this statement is either an idiot or a new chat room user, since anyone else would know that this statement is "passé" among the upper crust of chat room citizens.

AOL (abbr.) America On Line. syn: A O HELL, Assholes On Lithium.

Avatar (noun): a graphical symbol or image used to personify and identify an individual's presence in a chat room. Avatars are generally felt to possess the same degree of veracity as a profile or a screen name (see below).

B

BBL (abbr.): Be Back Later, a warning that the chatter will return at some indefinite time in the future (I'll BBL). It may also be used to indicate that a person is temporarily absent but expected to return (e.g. Daisy is BBL).

BBW (abbr.): Big Bodied Woman, a politically correct way of saying "fat bitch", usually indicates the presence of a Bloated Beached Whale.

Boot, the (noun): being disconnected from a chat program for reasons that are never quite clear or the same in consecutive instances. Is also used as a verb (I was booted).

Booter (noun): a particularly obnoxious and immature species of chatter that utilizes small blocks of computer code to administer "the boot" to another chatter, generally used against another chatter (or even an entire chat room) that has failed to respond to his particularly obnoxious, crude and definitely immature attempts at communication.

Bot (noun): a creation of the advertising world that, at first glance, appears to be just another chatter but is designed to trick the real (loosely defined as "human") chatter into logging into what is usually a porn site. If a human chatter is seen talking to a bot it generally means that chatter is either an idiot or is from some country where English is not spoken as the primary language. An alternative theory (although unsupported by evidence) holds that bots are the children of those that participate in unsafe *cyber-sex* (see below).

BRB (abbr.): Be Right Back. May also be interpreted as "Bath Room Break" if the chatter has been boozing it up, a fairly common event when in chat rooms.

Bug (noun): a section of computer software code that 1) does not work as expected and 2) is usually discovered only after the software is installed.

Broadband (noun): a generic term used to describe any form of Internet connection that transfers data at a speed greater than fifty-six thousand bits per second (56 kbps).

C

Cam (noun): a device that, when connected to a personal computer (*PC*, below) allows the user to broadcast live images of himself or herself to anyone that has the courage to view them. This is not recommended for the faint of heart, easily nauseated, or in the documented absence of a dominant masochistic tendency.

Cam (verb): to use the above-described device to 1) redefine ugly, 2) frighten children and small animals, 3) further damage East-West foreign policy, or 4) remove all doubt that possession and use of a personal computer should require a license.

Cam to Cam (verb): a form of *cyber-sex* (see below) in which two individuals observe each other, thus proving beyond reasonable doubt that misery indeed loves company.

Cheeta (noun): a chat program that allows a chatter to be obnoxious in more than one chat room simultaneously.

Christian Chat Room (misnomer): a chat room that was originally intended as a place for the adherents of Christianity to meet and discuss topics of common interest. Like other chat rooms, it has degenerated into something that even God would have trouble describing.

Cyber (verb): 1) Colloquial shortening of the term cyber-sex, used to indicate participation in the practice of that unique art form or, 2) a prefix used to denote that the combined words are to be taken as related to the Internet.

Cyber-sex (noun): a beneficial creation of the Internet era which allows lower life forms to mate without causing further contamination of the gene pool.

D

Dial-up (noun): a form of Internet connection involving the use of a telephone line. It is faster than the Pony Express but slower than two empty paper cups and a few miles of string. Dial-up connections tend to be less stable than Charlie Manson but are superior to blindly yelling out of a window.

Doofus (noun, masc.): a species of chatter that, although having the IQ of a golf ball, is not maliciously stupid but rather charmingly ignorant.

Doofette (noun, fem.): a female *doofus*

Drive-by (noun): a species of *bot* that makes a sudden appearance, posts some idiotic message, and then disappears.

E

E-mail (noun): in theory, a form of communication that involves sending messages via computer networks to individuals. In practice, the favored medium for the exchange of pornography and the transmission of computer viruses.

Ears (noun): the presence of speakers or a headset, a necessity if you (for some obscure reason) wish to participate in that form of intellectual masturbation known as *voice chat.*

ESL (abbr): English as a Second Language, an appropriate (and highly likely) descriptor of a significant number of chat room denizens, particularly those that are fond of the term *A/S/L*.

F

FAQ (noun): *Frequently Asked Questions*, a list of questions that commonly arise when installing new software, using a new computer, or some other task with the potential to be confusing or prone to user error. The FAQ are usually put together by support personnel to 1) save the customer time and trouble or 2) save the support staff from dealing with customers that should not have been allowed near a computer in the first place.

Flame (verb): to publish, send, transmit, or otherwise promote the practice of burying an individual beneath a mountain of derogatory and insulting e-mail or some other form of computer-assisted communications regardless of what that individual may (or may not) have done to warrant such a response.

G

Gag (noun): something that should be shoved into the mouth of every idiot using voice chat.

Geocities.com (noun): a subsidiary of *Yahoo* (see below) that has provided the "global village" of the *Internet* (see below) with a red light district.

H

Hai (unknown): a term used to indicate that the chatter is from *Obscuristan* or some other third world country that provides its citizens with computers, but not running water. The exact origin and definition of this term is unknown, but current scholarly research favors Sanskrit for the former and "I wish to be sodomized by the syphilitic goat" for the latter.

I

ICQ (abbr.): an acronym, supposedly a homonym for "I Seek You," a sophisticated chat program that allows its users to manage all their other chat programs, e-mail accounts, passwords etc. from one location and is thus well beyond the intellectual capability of the average chatter.

Idiot (noun): a generic term used to identify a substantial percentage of chat room denizens.

Iggy (colloq. form of Ignore): Used in conversational reference to the "Ignore Button," which itself is either a blessing or a bane, depending on if one is the "Iggy-or" or the Iggy-ee."

IM (abbr.): Instant Message, a way for two chatters to communicate in private, thus denying the rest of the chat universe the chance to learn what the two parties have been up to. IM is also a device used by people with no concept of politeness to pester other users with messages that almost always begin with "*A/S/L*?"

J

Jesus-pimp (noun): a practitioner of the Christian faith that, having dedicated its life to Jesus, has vowed to become a source of irritation to those that have not yet suffered a similar psychotic event.

K

K (abbr.): OK, acknowledge, understand, etc.

L

LMAO (abbr.): Laughing My Ass Off, a response to the rare event of someone saying an unusually funny remark but commonly used when another chatter has made an unusually prominent fool of themselves.

LMFAO (abbr.): Laughing My F______g Ass Off, an extreme response to the not so extremely rare event of another chatter making a spectacular fool of themselves.

LOL (abbr.): Laughing Out Loud, a milder response than "*LMAO*." In some instances it may be defined to mean "Loser, Oh Loser," particularly when the subject of the response has attempted to initiate a conversation with the expression "*A/S/L*."

M

Mad Cow Disease virus (noun): the only virus that has yet to be transmitted by e-mail, much to the regret of any chatter that has received a message beginning with "*Hai!! A/S/L*"

Mic (colloquial abbr.) a microphone, a vital tool when one wishes to be obnoxious in *voice chat*.

Moron (noun): synonymous with *Idiot*.

MUD (abbr.): Internet shorthand for Multiple User Dialog, a primitive form of chat in which one assumed a more or less permanent identity and engaged in cyber-activities that closely mimicked reality. MUDs required that the participants have both personalities and a certain minimal technical familiarity with computers and was thus far above the intellectual lever of 95% of computer owners. Naturally, MUDs became extinct within weeks of the creation of chat rooms.

N

Net, the (noun): see *Internet*.

O

Obscuristan (prop. noun): A generic name for a hopefully mythical third-world country well-known for the export of rude, obnoxious chat room users. Obscuristan's exact location is not known because no one has the stomach to go looking for it.

OMG (abbr.): Oh My God, an expression of shock or disbelief so great that the chatter is forced to seek the intervention of the Judeo-Christian God or some other deity not normally found in a chat room.

P

PC (abbr.): Personal Computer, the device that allows one to use the Internet for every possible situation except its original purpose.

PM (abbr.): Private Message, a synonym for *IM* and abused with the same frequency.

Political Chat Room (noun): a chat room dedicated to the debate of all things political and/or civic, usually in the most uncivil manner possible.

Profile (noun): Ideally, a place where chatters can post descriptions of themselves, describe their hobbies, and even post a picture of themselves. In practice, the biggest collection of lies since the most recent election.

Q

Queer Corner (noun): a gay and/or lesbian chat room.

R

R (abbr.): a symbol that often replaces the word "are" and most often used by Trolls (see below) or idiots (see above) in questions such as "how r u?"

R/L (abbr.): chat room shorthand for "real-life" or the phrase "in R/L," with both definitions being adequate to describe a social situation that is essentially absent in most chat room users.

RPG (abbr.): a shorthand reference to "Role Playing Game," a practice in which several delusional chatters combine their fantasies in order to attempt a mass breakout from the prison of reality.

ROFLMFAO (abbr.): Rolling On the Floor Laughing My F______g Ass Off. A term reserved for either 1) recognition of an unusually accurate observation or pithy remark or 2) to acknowledge a chatter that has reached a level of idiocy previously thought to be unattainable.

S

Screen Name (noun): the name by which the chatter is known, generally as truthful in describing the chatter as is the *profile page*.

Smiley (noun): a generic form of an avatar that is used to communicate information about the chatter's emotional state. There is apparently no truth to the rumor that the next release of Yahoo Chat will include either the "Son of Sam" or the "Charlie Manson" smiley.

T

Troll (noun): a term once found only in children's stories and, in that context, used to describe a hideous, deformed creature that lived under bridges and subsisted on the flesh of unlucky travelers. In chat rooms, however, a troll thrives on harassing other (usually female) chatters with unsolicited Instant Messages (see *PM* or *IM*, above) that always include a vulgar request for sex. Although a complete study of this species has not been published in a reputable scientific journal, it is believed that chat room trolls bear a strong physical resemblance to the more traditional variety.

Troll (verb): to conduct oneself in the manner of a troll, for some unknown reason.

U

U (abbr.): a symbol that often replaces the pronoun "you" and is generally found within the dialects of the English language spoken by *Trolls* or as part of a *PM* that opens with a phrase similar to "Hai!!! U lak the sex???"

V

Virus (noun): a malicious computer program that is used by social outcasts, borderline personality types, and teenagers without even a hope of a normal social life to make as many people as possible miserable.

Voice (noun): A tool of Satan that allows the illiterate chatter to be just as obnoxious, if not more so, as anyone else in a chat room.

W

Wanna-be (noun): a chatter that has no obvious redeeming social values but still hangs around in a chat room with vain the hope of being accepted.

Web Cam (noun): see *Cam*

Weekend Warrior (noun): a chatter that is usually seen only on weekends, as this is the only time that the chatter's spouse/parent is absent, which is the only time the chatter is allowed near a functional computer.

X

X (symbol): a symbolic form of shorthand that traditionally, when combined with the symbol O, meant "hugs and kisses." Currently, a shorthand notation of "fondles and gropes."

Y

Yahoo.com (noun): a well-known provider of chat rooms, which are grouped by age, sex, degree of social pathology, favored form of deviant behavior, or level of intellectual development (syn: Yahell).

Z

Zoo (noun): traditionally, a place for the public display of wild animals captured in remote, exotic places. Currently, an appropriate synonym for chat room.

5.

Politics in Wonderland (It's a Conspiracy !)

Democracy is also a form of worship. It is the worship of Jackals by Jackasses.

H. L. Mencken

Are you one of those people who occasionally gets in the mood to start an argument with a total stranger over a subject about which neither of you are particularly knowledgeable but yet both of your opinions border on fanaticism?

If you are, I have some great news for you! Instead of having to get off your lazy rear end, find someone to argue with, and take a chance on getting your butt kicked into the next time zone there is a way for you to invite other opinionated self-righteous jerks like yourself into the safety of your very own home. I would like to introduce you to the corner of cyber-space known as the political chat room. But "chat" is not quite the right word to use in this context because "chat" implies a brief, polite conversation as opposed to the arguments you encounter here, which are usually held at the yell and scream levels.

Political chat rooms are much like any of the other chat rooms in that they allow you to meet like-minded people to discuss topics of mutual interest. The similarity ends there. These rooms were envisioned as the reinvention of the Roman Forum, a place where the average citizen of the Empire could go to hear debates on important issues of the day. There are, of course, some important differences.

The first thing to remember is that the Roman Empire is deader than Elvis, and what killed it was that no one could agree on what to do next. They were great at talking and planning but eventually the Empire was overrun by a group of nomads that had never seen a paved road before, much less an organized debate. The disorganization of government that resulted did not die out completely. It can still be seen in the Roman Empire's mummified corpse, Italy, a country with more political parties than there are special interest groups in the US Congress combined with the stability of the San Andreas Fault.

You should also remember that in the days when Rome was the big dog on the known-world block it was common for the senators and other government officials to visit the Forum daily to meet with the citizens and hear their complaints. Can you even imagine an elected official visiting a chat room? Can you even imagine one showing up at anything other than a $250 a plate fund-raiser? Most of the incumbents are too busy sending e-mails asking for donations to their respective pet political action committees, which will then launder the money before donating it to the distinguished gentleman's or gentle-lady's campaign funds. Those who are seeking to take the incumbents' jobs have contingency plans in place to accomplish the same thing but are less obvious about it.

The denizens of political chat rooms seen to fall into distinct categories as in any of other rooms, with both sides of the political fence being about equally represented. What sets these particular chatters apart are the fervor of their beliefs (like the fundamentalist Christians) and the intensity of their dislike for anyone not smart enough to agree with them (another fundamentalist Christian trait). Working from right to left, let's take a look at some of these groups.

Over on the right you can usually find most of the stereotypes people associate with redneck gun-owning fascists from Texas or the Revs. Falwell and Robinson. This is the corner of the ring that believes "If it ain't in the Bible, it ain't true." They justify things like automobiles, television, air conditioning and other modern conveniences by saying, "If the damn Jews hadn't killed Jesus he would have mentioned them later." In their minds (such as those might be) all the troubles in the world are due to a dark cabal of Jews, liberals, blacks, the Council on Foreign Relations or some other as yet to be discovered group(s) that are sworn to destroy the white man and to giving Texas back to Mexico.

In the center of the ring are the moderates, people who just want to sit back and hear both sides of the debate and form their own opinions based on what is best for society as a whole and not what is best for them. These people tend to be well educated, have middle to upper-middle class lifestyles, and most have a college degree. At last count, there were twenty-seven people identified as belonging to this group.

Fighting out of the blue corner are the liberal Democrats, Socialists, and the last three people on Earth that still believe Communism works. This mob is only interested in taxing to death anyone who lives above the poverty level, although they would like to see the poverty level raised to whatever income level that would include them. They believe that everything from the extinction of the dinosaurs to the Yankees' loss in the World Series is due to a conspiracy between Big Business, the military-industrial complex, and people who own guns in general and handguns in particular. This corner is almost entirely populated by aging hippies, college freshmen, mental defectives, tree-hugging fish-kissing environmentalists, the entire Kennedy family and other varieties of social parasites.

Please be sure to remember that the above classifications are only guidelines and are not to be taken as all-inclusive. There are numerous chatters on line that do not fit into any of these categories. In fact, a lot of political chatters do not fit into any known subspecies of primates or any pathological process identified and recognized by the American Psychiatric Association.

Now that you have some idea what type of person inhabits a political chat room and the history of politics, let's take a look at how what is said is often colored by the chatter's core beliefs. Please note that the numbers preceding each chatter's name are for reference only, although they do save me from having to type the same line of mindless drivel twice.

1. *me:* what does everyone think about invading Iraq?

2. *real_american_patriot:* bomb the rag head shits into the stone age!

3. *vietnam_vet:* the friggin' camel-rapers are already in the stone age!

4. *gore_was_robbed:* just another trick by bush and cheney to cover up for their buddies at enron!

5. *greenpieces:* Bush doesn't protect the environment

6. *me:* what the hell does the environment have to do with saddam building atom bombs?

7. *idiot:* HAI!! a/s/l please

8. *vietnam_vet :* screw the environment and you too, chicken shit tree hugger!

9. *gore_was_robbed:* just another trick by bush and cheney to cover up for their buddies at enron!

10. *idiot:* hai, i am from Obscuristan

gore_was_robbed: conservatives are a bunch of Nazis and Bush is another Hitler

But what does all this really mean? Line #1 is a simple question and, more importantly, relevant to the national dialog at the time this essay was being written. Given that the national dialog has more twists and turns than a Colorado mountain road while simultaneously being as indecipherable as a Herman Hesse novel, things might have changed by the time you read this. For the sake of simplicity we will assume the question is still non-rhetorical.

Lines #2 and #3 are the typical responses from the right, but it can be misleading to put too much faith in the veracity of screen names. If you have read "Chat Rooms In Wonderland," you know that the majority of screen names are nothing but so much cyber-crap. This is usually the case with the right wing of the political chat room. Most of those who claim to be combat veterans, law enforcement officers or other such macho types would wet their pants in terror if ever forced to confront an armed adversary. Although their responses seem to make the most sense I would hesitate to make a decision based on the advice of someone that gets their combat experience from watching HBO.

The left weighs in with its opinion in lines #4, #5 and #9. The screen name of gore_was_robbed tells us that this crybaby can't accept that Gore lost, plain and simple, and continues to whine the mantra of sore losers such as Joe Lieberman and Dan Rather. By attempting to link a potential invasion of another country with a domestic scandal this chatter also demonstrates his total lack of an alternative course of action as well as showing his (or her) inability to do any type of intellectual activity that cannot be duplicated by a well-trained Myna bird. But I would like to call your attention to line #9.

This is a favorite ploy for anyone who, having run out of arguments in support of their position (by either having them disproved or by those arguments collapsing under the weight of their inherent stupidity) attempts to "paint with a wide brush" anyone who disagrees with them as Nazis. This last-stand technique was first documented in the days prior to the Internet Age (pre-1995) in *Godwin's Law* which is named in honor of Mike Godwin who, in the early 1990s, made the discovery that appears below (paraphrased to include the Internet Era phenomenon known as a chat room):

> "As a chat room discussion grows longer (*T*), the probability (*P*) of a comparison involving Nazis or Hitler approaches one."

Or, in mathematical terms:

$$P\text{Nazi} + P\text{Hitler} \quad 1.0 \text{ as } T$$

In all fairness, the foundation for Godwin's Law was laid over forty years earlier, in Leo Strauss's 1950 book *Natural Right and History*:

> "In following this movement towards its end we shall inevitably reach a point beyond which the scene is darkened by the shadow of Hitler. Unfortunately, it does not go without saying that in our examination we must avoid the fallacy that in the last decades has frequently been used as a substitute for the *reductio ad absurdum*: the *reductio ad Hitlerum*. A view is not refuted by the fact that it happens to have been shared by Hitler."

As noted above and in the chapter "Religion in Wonderland" the majority of chat room denizens are more than willing to give you their opinion on practically any subject, particularly those subjects on which they are the least knowledgeable.

This behavior was successfully predicted in what we now know as *Benford's Law of Controversy*, which was originally proposed by its discoverer Gregory Benford in 1980. This well-known law states:

> "Passion is inversely proportional to the amount of real information available."

Or, as an alternative form of the Tooth/Tattoo Ratio (see "Chat Rooms in Wonderland"):

> "The passion and frequency with which an opinion is stated is inversely proportional to the IQ of the speaker."

Vox Populi

And yes, there is something called "voice" available in most political chat rooms and it is used almost exclusively by the same class of chatters that have embraced it so warmly in other rooms. That is to say, the chatters that are functional illiterates make use of voice to demonstrate their complete lack of any redeeming social qualities that would justify placing them on life support for longer than thirty seconds.

And if you think voice chatters are annoying in other chat rooms, get ready to join a monastery and take a vow of silence after spending a few minutes around the baying jackasses that use political chat as their grazing ground. This is a truly democratic process in that you can find loudmouthed idiots from all parts of the political spectrum who haven't the slightest idea what they're talking about being as equally represented as their literate counterparts. And regardless of the topic of discussion in any given chat room, it won't take long for some off the wall conspiracy theory to be brought up.

The White Picket Fence on a Grassy Knoll Theory of Everything

It seems that the American public will believe anything as long as it is presented as a component of a conspiracy theory. Pick up any popular tabloid at the supermarket checkout line and you will find the latest news concerning the escape of the space alien from a super-secret Area Something or Another, or the "inside story" on how the government is trying to cover up "the truth" behind its latest colossal blunder (note to self: check with editor to see if it's permissible to say "truth" and "government" on the same page). Whatever your political, social, religious beliefs happen to be I can assure you that there is at least one alleged conspiracy involved.

The "mother of all conspiracy theories" is undoubtedly the family of speculations that surround the assassination of President Kennedy in 1963. Over the decades since that November day the "investigations" into "the cover up" have blossomed into a cottage industry that has produced no fewer than eight million-selling books, three documentaries, two full-length movies, and two congressional select committees. For those not familiar with this particular conspiracy, let me summarize by lumping all of the theories into a single paragraph.

> President Kennedy was shot by at least eight people firing from twelve different locations, with at least three of them firing from behind a white picket fence atop a grassy knoll while being invisible to each other. The shooters had been assembled by a conspiracy involving the most unlikely alliance since the fall of the

> Roman Empire, including the CIA, the mafia, the military-industrial complex, Fidel Castro, Nikita Khrushchev, Lyndon Johnson, J. Edgar Hoover, and the cow that jumped over the moon.

If the above description seems a little incredulous, I invite you to consider the following "urban legends," to use the more socially-acceptable term for what were once known as "outright lies."

> Crack cocaine was invented by the CIA as a method of genocide directed against urban African-Americans.
>
> The AIDS virus was created by the same to be used for the same purpose.
>
> The attacks of September 11, 2001 were planned by a Zionist cabal whose intent was to inflame American public opinion into an anti-Arab frenzy that Israel would exploit in its constant efforts to persecute Muslims.

If We Don't Get These Anarchists Organized...

The United States has, for the most part, always had two major political parties. Although there have been numerous attempts to form other parties, these have generally failed to attract a substantial following due to their inability to provide anything close to a reasonable alternative to the status quo or even come up with a candidate with a clean psychiatric bill of health. In addition, don't forget that third parties are usually composed of third-rate citizens as well.

Both the major parties, the Democrats and the Republicans, claim to be closest to the original beliefs of the "founding fathers", although the Democrats are trying to distance themselves from this term due to pressure from the Feminist lobby which feels that this "sexist" term does not reflect the contribution of women to the early history of the Nation. This is an appropriate response because the Democratic Party is also trying to distance itself from the Constitution, the history books, and anything that remotely resembles Democracy.

At the same time the Democrats are advocating racial and sexual quotas, the concept that an individual's actions are the result of a racist society and therefore the individual is a "victim" and cannot be held accountable, and erasing from public view any form of religious expression that might compete with the notion that all truth and righteousness originates within the Democratic Party. Throw in a few more idiots like Jesse Jackson, Hillary Clinton, and Ted Kennedy (actually any Kennedy of either sex will do) and you have the party that will lead you into the Welfare State Promised Land.

If you don't consider things like common sense or the rights of the individual important, there is no real difference between the Democratic and Republican parties. If you happen to value these archaic notions, then there is one Hell of a difference. The Republicans think that the best thing that central government can do for the citizens of the Republic is to get out of the way and leave them alone because the individual, they believe, will work for the improvement of their own situation and therefore become less reliant on handouts from the rest of the taxpayers as distributed by the government.

Republicans believe that if you lower tax rates the individual will have more money to spend, or invest, which will lead to a healthy economy because a robust economy means that there will be more jobs created or opened up for those with the skills and/or education required for those jobs.

Republicans also believe that success is something that should be rewarded and not be considered as a sign that someone else has been "exploited", a favorite claim of the Democrats who think that success is evil because we should all "share and share alike" (unless you are a Democrat or one of their mouthpieces in the entertainment industry).

Americans, who generally do not like to engage in intensive cerebral activity, have always filled their political campaigns with references to such as things as "the religious right," "leftist economic policy," "conservative politician," or "liberal voting record" In fact, it has become difficult for me to remember the time when either "Democratic" or "Republican" was the only adjective needed to identify a politician's position on any issue placed before the voting public. Surprisingly, adjectives such as "liberal" or "conservative" are not recent additions to the political dictionary but instead have a rather interesting genealogy.

The use of generic terms to describe a candidate's general political philosophy can be traced back to the year 1679 and the heated debate within the English Parliament over whether to exclude, because he was a Roman Catholic, the future King James II from succession to the throne. Those who favored a strong Parliament and a non-Catholic monarch became known as "Whigs," which was taken from a Scottish word that meant (among other things) "horse thief." If you were loyal to the monarchy you were known a "Tory," a word derived from the Irish term for "Catholic outlaw," which is what James II became after being the guest of honor during the "Glorious Revolution" of 1688.

In fact, it was these same debates that introduced "right" and "left" as political descriptors. The Tories, being loyal to tradition and thus conservative when it came to political and social changes, sat as a group on the right side of the aisle than ran through the Parliament chambers while their Whig adversaries congregated to the left of that aisle. It is not known whether the absence of seats in the aisle itself was due to the fact that there were no "centrists" in those days or if politicians had yet to discover that they raid the public treasury for money to buy such essentials as comfortable chairs.

Not all political adjectives have such distinguished histories. I grew up in what was once known as the "Solid South," a term that arose from the tendency of the states that had made up the old Confederacy to vote for any candidate that wasn't a Republican. Which brings to mind the colorful descriptor "yellow dog" Democrat to denote someone who would proudly state that they would "vote for a yellow dog if it ran as a Democrat."

All things being equal, I am more certain than ever that the original definitions of conservatives (Tory) and liberals (Whig) cannot be improved upon. In 2004, "outlaws" and "horse thieves" seems more appropriate with each passing day.

There are, of course, many more differences between the two parties. I will not even to bother to attempt to list them all because anyone with an IQ above room temperature already knows the differences. The Democrats would not be able to understand the explanations anyway, because most cannot read and write above grade school level and it is very hard to find pictures that they can understand, much less color with their crayons.

As I mentioned earlier there have been numerous attempts to form other political parties in the United States, all of which must be considered as failures since none has ever attracted enough voters to be taken seriously by anyone other than themselves. This does not mean that these parties have been without influence and in fact they have changed the political and social history of the nation, but they always did so totally by accident. Consider the following examples:

> In 1948 the States Rights (Dixiecrats) Party, under Strom Thurmond of South Carolina, pulled enough votes away from President Harry Truman that challenger Tom Dewey came very close to unseating the Democratic incumbent. The Democratic Party heaped praise onto the American public for having the common sense to re-elect Truman. This election, and the gloating behavior of the Democrats, set the stage for the Republican landslide victory of 1952 (along

> with launching the national political career of an obscure California congressman named Richard Nixon).
>
> In 1992 an egotistical Texan named Ross Perot launched a third-party candidacy for President. Despite making a total fool of himself, he managed to draw enough voters away from incumbent President George H. Bush to give the election to challengers Bill and Hillary Clinton. The Democratic Party hailed this event as proof that the American people had spoken and that the American Constitution was the best political document ever written by mortal man.
>
> The shoe was on the other foot in the 2000 election, when Ralph Nader and the Green Party pulled enough votes away from Democrat Al Gore to give the election to Republican George W. Bush. The Democratic Party called this conclusive proof that the Constitution was a flawed document and should be rewritten as soon as possible, that the American people had actually wanted Gore to win but weren't smart enough to mark the right spot on a ballot, and that third parties were the bane of freedom-loving people all over the known universe.

Do you somehow get the impression that the Democratic Party wants to play by the rules only if the rules allow them to win?

This brings us to the "crucial" election year of 2004, the election that the Democrats swore would mark the return of power to the American people and the overthrow of the "appointed" Bush administration. By sunrise on November 3, 2004 the Democratic Party was in shock: Those damned voters still didn't know what was good for them and had given the election to that source of all evil which, as all "compassionate citizens" knew, was George W. Bush.

How could this be? Surely, the party thought, the American people wanted to elect Kerry. But why didn't the votes show a Kerry victory? Was it because the people had made an intelligent choice? Of course not! If the voters made an intelligent choice, then Kerry was on his way to the White House and the Democrats could start planning their revenge on everyone who had opposed them in their failed *coup d' etat* four years previously. Obviously, something was very wrong here.

The Democratic Party (and a soon to be unemployed news-hack named Dan Rather) was now in the same condition as Dresden in May of 1945: a burned-out shell of its former self with no prospects for immediate recovery. Obviously, there had to be a logical explanation for the drubbing that their best and brightest candidate, the "heir to Camelot," had just taken. Although there are no copies of the innumerable memos and e-mails that must have been circulating at party headquarters that morning, they probably looked something like this:

TO: All National Committee Staff

FROM: Director, Ministry of Truth

SUBJECT: What the F__k Happened?

As all of you (at least those of you that are still here) are aware, things did not go as well as we had hoped yesterday. This will, of course, require a downsizing of out staff at the national level. But before the pink slips begin, we must find out why our candidate got his ass kicked! The Ministry has put together the following list of potential explanations with a brief listing of the pros and cons regarding each of them.

Let's get to work people, since none of us will be sleeping in the Lincoln bedroom any time soon. Do any of you look forward to another four years of daily, whining telephone calls from Barbara Streisand?

We lost, plain and simple, in a fair election.

Pro

This is the simplest explanation. We can just admit it and then start working on getting Hillary elected in 2008.

Con

No way! We're the Party of the People, even if the People are too stupid to know what the people want.

The voters in Florida didn't know how to use the ballots.

Pro

We've been saying this at least twice a day for the last four years, so it should be familiar to everyone.

Con

No one has believed it after four years. Why should they believe it now?

Kerry's wife sounded too much like Eva Peron.

Pro

It's true.

Con

What does truth have to do with any of this?

Then it dawned on the party Pooh-Bahs and excuse-makers: there was a conspiracy at work here! A conspiracy of the evil right-wingers, fundamentalist Christians, gun owners, and others demonstrating similar forms of social pathologies had stolen the election that had been divinely ordained as belonging to the Democratic Party!

A Conspiracy!! Now that one we can sell to a public that has trouble reading a stop sign!

TO: All National Committee Staff

FROM: Director, Ministry of Truth

SUBJECT: Official Party Line Explaining Yesterday's Fiasco

After a detailed investigation of certain anomalies in the voting patterns of several key states in yesterday's election, the Ministry of Truth has determined that a conspiracy of dangerous right-wing reactionary elements has stolen the Presidential election from the people's rightful choice, John Kerry, and given control of the government to that tool of the Capitalists and the Religious Right, George W. Bush.

The Ministry of Truth suggests that all citizens who supported the People's candidate, Senator Kerry, immediately move to Canada and bask in its wonderful socialist atmosphere while the Ministry selects a candidate for the next election that will be able to parrot our Progressive message to the People while keeping a straight face.

Isn't it such a lovely touch of irony that the symbol of the Democratic Party is a jackass?

At the beginning of this section I made mention that America seems to be in love with conspiracy theories. This isn't all that surprising when you stop to consider what a conspiracy theory does for the individual. The central selling point of many conspiracies is, quite simply, that such theories relieve the individual of the onerous burden self-accountability.

As an example consider one of the more successful conspiracy theories, communism.

The central tenet of communism is that the wealthy conspire actively to oppress the non-wealthy and that it is only the power of the state keeps the non-wealthy "in their place," where they must work at menial, low wage jobs to benefit the wealthy. Therefore, since the state is for the benefit of the rich and powerful the only hope that the non-wealthy have is to gain control of the state by revolution.

But since revolutions, historically, have tended to be pretty messy things followed by a few years of hardships where a lot of people are either killed outright or die of starvation, maybe the revolution thing isn't exactly what we want either. Maybe if we elect people who promise to help us out, we can get what we want at the expense of the evil capitalists who have been oppressing us!

What a conspiracy theory actually says is, quite simply, that the individual has to take no accountability for their own decisions because society "conspires" to make their lives miserable. Quit school in the ninth grade because it was cutting into your social life and now you can't read the "Help Wanted" ads in the newspaper? No problem! Nobody will hire you because your criminal record is longer than the employment application? No problem! It's because there's a conspiracy at work against you! Just elect me to ______________ and I'll take care of you by taxing everyone else so you can get even with those nasty, rich conspirators.

Just stop, for a moment, and reflect on how much of our national social policies are based on "correcting" some "injustice" that is supposedly the result of some "conspiracy."

Scary thought, isn't it?

Another nice thing about conspiracy theories is that once formulated and proposed, conspiracy theories are unique in that they need absolutely none of the routine intellectual maintenance that other, less exotic ideas such as the Theory of Evolution or the Theory of Relativity periodically require. Conspiracy theories make such great explanations for just about anything simply because you never have to produce any data in support of them. If someone asks you for proof of your latest-discovered conspiracy, all you have to say in your defense is "I can't prove it, because the evidence is being suppressed by the conspiracy."

And if you think I'm making that up just for your entertainment, drop in on the political chat rooms some day when you are ready to have your last vestiges of faith in the goodness of humanity ripped into shreds and tossed out the nearest window.

6.

A Political Dictionary for Our Times

If there's one thing I can't stand, it's intolerance.
(Author Unknown)

A

Abortion (noun) : a medical procedure that is opposed by those that object to the taking of a human life and supported by those who are against capital punishment. Alt. Def: a form of proactive capital punishment.

Acting (noun): a profession that has consistently produced a better quality governor of the State of California.

Activist (noun): one seeking to promote either a personal or a group agenda by being as obnoxious as is humanly possible.

Affirmative Action (noun): a program that encourages the inclusion of the marginal by means of discrimination against the competent.

Animal Rights (noun): the theory that the Founding Fathers intended the Constitution to include non-human animals and theses Constitutional Rights are to be protected by any means necessary, up to and including killing humans.

Antichrist (noun): the ultimate bad guy as described in the oldest-known science fiction story, the *Revelation of John*. Alternatively, an honorary title used by Evangelicals to describe an incumbent Democratic president.

B

Bill of Rights (noun): that portion of the American Constitution which is used in place of toilet paper by the FBI, the Internal Revenue service, and the Department of Homeland Security.

Biodiversity (noun): a mantra of the Environmentalist movement that is repeated often to demonstrate one's fanatical devotion to the belief that the road to Nirvana is a foot path through an old growth forest.

Biosphere (noun): that portion of the physical world inhabited by animal rights activists, environmentalists, various and sundry socially maladapted individuals, and the junior senator from New York.

Blue State (noun): an invention of the television news industry that denotes a state whose voters favored the Democratic candidate. This term has been very useful in that it saves the viewer the mental anguish involved when attempting to read and understand the numbers presented.

Bork (verb): to attack a person, particularly a nominee to a position requiring Congressional approval, by using unsubstantiated statements (lies) regarding the person's qualifications.

Bork, Robert (noun): former Appeals Court judge and Supreme Court nominee who has attained some degree of immortality by having his surname converted to a verb by the Senate Judiciary Committee after having his fitness for the Court questioned, on national television, by Ted Kennedy.

Bureaucracy (noun): the most inefficient and potentially corrupt form of government and thus actively supported by both parties.

Business, Big (noun): a loose and poorly-defined group that, with the *Military-Industrial Complex*, the *Republican Party*, and *Big Oil,* form the root of all evil.

C

Camelot (noun): a Broadway musical that was adapted to the political stage and featured *Jack Kennedy* as King Arthur and Lyndon Johnson as Mordred.

Capital Punishment (noun): a practice that is condemned as barbaric by those favoring abortion and supported as a social necessity by those opposed to abortion. Alt def: a retroactive abortion.

Capitol Punishment (noun): that which is administered to the losing party after an election by the winning party.

Carter, Jimmy (noun): the last *Democrat* to have served as President prior to Bill Clinton and is now best known for building houses that are considerably stronger than most of his decisions while in office. Carter is also the first and possibly only President to have made only one campaign promise (I'll never lie to you") and then keep that promise. He was rewarded with being defeated, in a landslide, by *Ronald Reagan.*

CBS (noun): the publicity department of the Democratic Party. Alternatively, the Clinton Bombastic System.

Center (noun): that portion of the political spectrum that is not in favor of (or opposed to) anything.

*Centrist (*noun): one that embraces the center position as a consequence of apathy.

Christianity (noun): a rowdy and vocal mob that excels at both distorting and ignoring the teachings of its namesake.

Christmas (noun): a seasonal event that is used by the Religious Right in a yearly attempt to break down the Holy Wall of Separation between Church and State.

Class Struggle (noun): the central thesis of the discredited economic theory known as *Communism* that has been rechristened as Class Warfare and adopted as a central thesis of the *Democratic Party.*

Clinton, Bill (noun): a member of the Living Trinity of the *Democratic Party*, a deity that that descended from Mount Olympus to lead the Chosen People out of the dreaded desert known as the Twelve Years of Reagan/Bush.

Clinton, Hillary (noun): Olympian Goddess, second member of the Living Trinity of the *Democratic Party*, and spouse of *Bill Clinton* that descended from the Mount with him and is currently awaiting a direct order from God to lead the Chosen People out of the great desert known as the Eight Years of George W. Bush.

Conservative (noun): one who believes that, irrespective of what the magnitude of the problem may be, more taxes and more government regulations are not the solution.

Constitution (noun): a document that has outlived its usefulness to the point that it is ignored by Congress and no longer a required subject in law schools.

Communist (noun): an endangered species.

Communism (noun): an extinct (although not quite dead yet) political and economic system that combined the worst ideas of the previous four thousand years of human history and forced it onto the citizens at gunpoint.

Compassion (noun): favoring the use of the taxpayers' money for everything except the benefit of the taxpayers.

Creation Science (misnomer): the latest attempt by the Religious Right to shove their Bronze Age superstitious nonsense down the throats of schoolchildren of all faiths.

D

Democrat (noun): one that upholds the beliefs of the Democratic Party, mindlessly parrots its beliefs, and mindlessly follows its commands.

Democratic Party (noun): a group of professional victims that have dedicated themselves to championing every illogical or irrational idea that has ever been proposed. Its symbol is a jackass.

Diversity (noun): that which is guaranteed by the use of Affirmative Action and other similar programs which seek to insure the broadest possible range of mediocrity.

Discrimination (noun): a policy that is to be attacked when used as a tactic by your opponent and praised when used by those supporting you.

E

Economics (noun): a form of witchcraft whose practitioners claim 100% accuracy in making the wrong guess.

Elephant (noun): The symbol of the Republican Party, an organization that proudly notes the fact that when Hannibal attacked Rome during the Punic War he did so on elephants and not jackasses.

Endangered Species (noun): a species that, having either outlived its biological usefulness or by failing to adapt in response to a changing environment, is attempting to self-destruct.

Environmentalist (noun): one who believes that Charles Darwin's ideas concerning natural selection were wrong and tirelessly works to prevent nature from applying them.

Evangelical (noun): a particularly dangerous species of Christian that is 1) believed to be incapable of engaging in anything resembling a calm discussion of an issue and 2) has been predicting the immediate Second Coming of Jesus Christ for the last thirty years.

F

Fascist (noun): a generic term used by members of the Democratic Party to describe anyone who either is not a member of the Party or does not support its agenda.

Florida (noun): a state used by the Republican Party to steal the 2000 election from a candidate with even less charisma than the 2004 candidate.

Focus on the Family (noun): a collection of idiots under the leadership of idiot-in-chief James Dobson, a man noted for his God-given ability to detect homosexual conspiracies involving Sponge Bob and the Teletubbies.

Former (noun): an adjective used to identify a politician who, having lost an election, is actively plotting to regain public office.

Fox News Channel (noun): the publicity department of the Republican Party and mortal enemy of both the CBS and CNN news operations.

Freedom (noun): an outdated concept that assumes that the autonomy of the individual is superior to the will of State.

Freedom of Speech (noun): a concept that should be either supported or suppressed depending on whether or not you agree with the speaker is saying.

Freedom Fighter (noun): a terrorist devoted to any cause that you happen to support.

G

God (noun): a generic term that defines one's concept of a supreme being who is, invariably, on both sides of any given argument. Alternatively, the person or being that is blamed for everything but denied credit for anything beneficial.

GOP (noun): Grand Old Party, a synonym for the *Republican Party* and responsible for everything from the extinction of the dinosaurs to conspiracies to steal elections in which victories for Democratic candidates had been promised by no less than *God* Himself.

Goals (noun): synonym for quotas.

Green Party (noun): a minor political party composed of minor voters supporting the most mediocre candidates available.

Gun Control (noun): a term that means elimination of all means of self-defense when used by a Democratic candidate and being able to hit who or what you're shooting at when made by a Republican.

H

Hate Crime (noun): the portion of the Criminal Code that has been enacted into law that gives special status to certain members of society but not to the general public, invariably given as a reward to those groups whose members have supported the proper political party.

Hate Speech (noun): anything said in deviation from the official party line or in support of your opponent.

History (noun): that portion of the social, political, and economic record of society that is revised and rewritten annually in a futile attempt to please everyone.

House of Representatives (noun): the junior body of the United States Congress where potential candidates for higher offices learn the art of raiding the public treasury while avoiding testifying in one's own defense.

Humanism (noun): a philosophical system that is anathema to the Religious Right, who cite it as the root of all pain and suffering.

I

Inappropriate Decision (noun): a mistake brought about by one's own stupidity.

Infrastructure Building (noun): what occurs when the taxpayers' money is spent on useless projects inside your Congressional district.

Injustice (noun): that which has been committed when your candidate is defeated or you client is convicted.

Intolerance (noun): a term used to describe the attitude of someone that does not buy into the distorted logic behind your own beliefs.

J

Jackass (noun): the ultimate example of stubbornness, an appropriate symbol of the Democratic Party.

Jackson, Jesse (prop. noun): an egocentric activist for numerous causes in which he has either a personal or a vested financial interest.

Jury, Simpson (noun): a jury panel which proved, beyond any possibility of doubt, that if you look long enough you can find a dozen people that will believe anything.

K

Kennedy (prop. noun): the Blessed and Holy Family of the *Democratic Party* whose Patriarch was Joseph (Old Joe), who is best remembered for his role in supporting the appeasement policy of Chamberlain regarding Adolph Hitler. His sons were Young Joe (blown up during WW II), Jack (Martyr), Bobby (Martyr), and Ted (living, against all odds).

Kennedy, John F. (Jack): the first Martyr of the Blessed and Holy Kennedy Family, whose death lead directly to the rise of both Lyndon Johnson and the Vietnamese War.

Kennedy, Robert F. (Bobby): the second Martyr of the Blessed and Holy Kennedy family, whose death lead directly to the election of Richard Nixon.

Kennedy, Theodore F. (Ted): the only member of the Blessed and Holy Kennedy Family to have avoided Martyrdom and thus, with

Bill and Hillary Clinton, is the third member of the Living Trinity of the *Democratic Party*.

L

Lack of Compassion (noun): objecting to the use of the taxpayers' money to pay off various special interest groups.

Left (noun): the opposite of right.

Liberal (noun): one subscribing to the theory that there is no problem that cannot be solved through higher taxes, more intervention by the government, and the punishment of the innocent.

Libertarian Party (noun): the Republican Party on crystal methamphetamine.

M

Marx, Karl (prop. name): social outcast who wrote *The Communist Manifesto* and posthumously, a significant portion of the economic policy of the *Democratic Party*.

Military-Industrial Complex (noun): that part of the business community that is under the special protection of the Republican Party in return for generous campaign contributions and advice on when and where to send the next invasion force.

Moral Majority (noun): a subset of the Religious Right that is neither moral nor in the majority.

Morality (noun): a set of philosophical principles praised by all and implemented by none.

N

NEA (abbr.): (1) National Education Association, the academically-oriented part of the Labor Movement that is responsible for raising money and intimidating voters on behalf of the *Democratic Party*, or (2) National Endowment for the Arts, an organization dedicated to the use of tax dollars to support and promote incompetent writers and artists.

November 22 (noun): the Feast Day of Jack Kennedy (Martyr).

NPR (abbr.): National Public radio, a taxpayer-supported organization that is responsible for the production and broadcasting of such dry, boring programming that no sponsor would dare want associated with its name.

O

Ohio (noun): the state used by the Republican Party to steal the 2004 election from a candidate with the charisma of a drunken goat.

Oil (noun): the primary reason for having both a Department of Defense and a State Department.

Oil, Big (noun): an evil cabal that is behind the *Republican Party* and is responsible for global warming, starving children, landslides in the Chilean Andes Mountains and a host of yet to be discovered problems.

P

Political Science (noun): an oxymoron, as there is nothing scientific about politics.

Politics (noun): the methods and practices used to obtain access to the public treasury.

Pork-Barrel Spending (noun): *infrastructure-building* that occurs in a Congressional district other than your own.

Pro-Choice (noun): generally, anti-anything related to the conservative end of the political spectrum.

Pro-Life (noun): generally, anti-anything resembling common sense.

Propaganda (noun): any statement that touts the merits of your opponent's beliefs, record, or policies.

Q

Question (noun): in Politics, something that is to be evaded at all times.

Quota (noun): something that does not exist but is still in use.

R

Racist (noun): anyone that disagrees with, or does not actively support, the statements and programs of Jesse Jackson, Al Sharpton, or Charles Wrangle.

Reagan, Ronald (noun): either the greatest President of the United States or the source of every social ill in the world, depending on one's political beliefs.

Recount (noun): a more sophisticated method of stealing elections. It is to be supported as "vital to the electoral process" when your candidate wins and fought all the way to the Supreme Court if your candidate loses the initial election.

Recount (verb): to reexamine and retally all the votes until you are satisfied that your candidate has won.

Red State (noun): a state whose voters backed the Republican candidate, an invention of the television news industry, an industry that was already world-renowned for its ability to invent news as well.

Reform (noun): the act of changing the law as to maximize your position and inhibit those of your opponents.

Religious Right (noun): a loose confederation of religious zealots that is not well known for its open-minded dialog on any subject that has arisen in the course of history, the sworn enemy of both the Democratic Party and the Humanist movement.

Republican (noun): a supporter of the Republican Party.

Republican Party (noun): the political party that is often cited by Liberals as the source of every known evil at home and abroad.

Right (noun): see Left.

Rowe v Wade (noun): a Supreme Court decision that has, characteristically, decided nothing.

S

Second Hand Smoke (noun): an environmental hazard invented by the Environmental Protection Agency and a favorite complaint topic of second hand citizens to their second-hand congressmen and mayors.

Senate (noun): the senior body of the United States Congress composed of those who have excelled at raiding the public treasury while avoiding the attentions of a grand jury.

Social Security (noun): the most sacred member of the herd of scared cows.

Socialism (noun): a milder form of *Communism* in which the State runs the citizen's lives without waiting on instructions from the Party.

Special Interest Group (noun): a collection of various individuals, businesses, or others sharing a similar delusion that the very survival of the Republic is contingent upon their each and every wish being granted.

T

Terrorist (noun): a freedom fighter whose goals are different from those supported by you.

Theory (noun): The intermediate stage between superstition and wild guess.

Thomas, Clarence (noun): A Supreme Court Justice who was given "the equivalent of an electronic lynching" at his Senate confirmation hearing and was further humiliated when he was forced to sit quietly while his moral fitness for the position was questioned by Ted Kennedy and Joe Biden. It is not clear whether the latter act was considered to be "Cruel and Unusual" punishment.

Tolerance (noun): the act of accepting the unbelievably tortured reasoning behind your latest idiotic idea, statement, or explanation while refusing to hear any other statement that might refute or disprove it.

Trial by Jury (noun): A provision of the *Constitution* that, in theory, provides anyone accused of a crime a fair and impartial trial based on the evidence presented to it. However, there is no Constitutional mandate that this jury have a collective IQ above room temperature.

Trial of the Century (noun): this month's featured trial as presented by Court TV.

Truth (noun): Something that will always be found in your statements, actions, or policies but seldom, if ever, in those of your opponent.

U

Undocumented Immigrant (noun): Illegal alien.

Uniform (noun): an article of clothing that is absent in the wardrobes of the majority of members of Congress.

Union (noun): that branch of the Labor Movement whose primary function is to both raise money and intimidate voters on behalf of the *Democratic Party.*

V

Victory (noun): an outcome that has eluded the *Democratic Party* at home in elections and the *Republican* Party in military interventions abroad.

Viet Nam (noun): an insignificant country that was involved in a conflict that began under a Democratic administration and ended under a Republican administration, to the satisfaction of neither.

W

*War (*noun): historically, a much more effective form of foreign policy than diplomacy.

X

*X (*noun): formerly, a mark that was placed on a ballot to indicate one's choice in an election but is no longer used since, thanks to our enlightened educational policies, its use is above the intellectual capacity of most citizens.

Y

Yankee (noun): an American who is tolerated in the southern United States and despised by the rest of the world.

Z

Zoo (noun): a place, such as the United States Congress, that houses dangerous, predatory animals which are periodically placed on public display.

7.

Political Correctness in Wonderland

Since You've read this far, you might have gotten the idea that I'm not all that enthusiastic about people that have adopted what is commonly known as "political correctness" and its numerous incarnations such as "gender-neutral expression" (using no words that attach "values" or "preference" but rather using terms such as "she/he/it" which leads inevitably to the contraction "s/h/it"), "tolerance" (accepting all ideas as equally valid regardless of how idiotic they might be), and "social responsibility" (dedicating one's life to shoving every idiotic idea ever conceived down the throats of everyone that could care less).

When I started this book I began searching for a good definition of the word "satire." You might think that would be an easy thing to do: find a definition and copy it (after giving credit to the author, of course). If you think that's the case you are wrong to the extent that you automatically qualify for elective office on the national level! Trust me, it ain't that easy.

I learned many years ago that, as a general rule, the only way to challenge the validity of a given point was by determining if its thesis could survive examination by satiric ridicule. That is the plain and simple reason why this book exists. It is an attempt to have you, the reader, pause just long enough to appreciate the many follies of the blundering herd of which we find ourselves members.

As far as I'm concerned, there have only been four great satirists in the Western World in the last three hundred years: Jonathan Swift, Voltaire, Mark Twain, and George Orwell. Swift's explanation of satire, takes from the preface of his practically unknown *Battle of the Books* will explain why I feel that satire is most the noble literary genre.

> *Satyr* is a sort of Glass, wherein Beholders do *generall* discover every body's Face but their Own; which is the chief Reason for that kind of Reception it meets in the World, and that so very few are offended with it. But if it should happen otherwise, the Danger is not great; and, I have learned from long Experience, never to apprehend Mischief from those Understandings, I have been able to provoke; For, Anger and Fury, though they add Strength to the Sinews of the Body, yet are found to relax those of the Mind, and to render all its Efforts feeble and impotent.

Sadly, some users of the Internet are so impressed with themselves that they would be incapable of gazing into Swift's "Glass" without supplemental instructions, much less "discover every body's Face but their Own." If I may, a case in point.

I posted the following essay at one of the web sites that features all genres of writing, but emphasizes humorous essays and fiction.

Invited Commentary

Why I Smoke

By

Jeremiah Wazza-Boolphrogg, MD, PhD.

Emeritus Director,
The Robert Blake Handgun Safety Institute
North Hollywood, CA

It seems that not a single day can pass without your humble correspondent being bombarded with another round of reasons why I should not smoke cigarettes. And although these messages are well-intended and originate from different organizations or different individuals, all seem to have the same ultimate intention: to shame and/or scare me into not smoking (or use any type of tobacco products). And, like everyone else, I have heard all the reasons and been given all the facts that should have caused me to stop using tobacco long ago. But, as you might have guessed, I haven't stopped. Please allow me to explain the reasons behind why I continue to smoke.

Perhaps the greatest factor that causes me to continue to smoke is that I like it. Not only do I like to smoke I also happen to NOT like withdrawal symptoms, which is what I will develop if deprived of my cigarettes for any length of time. If you want to see an example of what John Gotti may have been like on a bad hair day, take away my cigarettes. And then run for cover, because after about two hours of nicotine deprivation I am not a pleasant person. This in no way implies that I am a pleasant person to begin with, but without my cigarettes I could easily become a role model for the Charlie Manson Chapter of the Future Mass Murderers of America.

Among the many reasons I have to continue smoking is that I feel it is my civic responsibility not only to smoke but to smoke as much as possible. The Centers for Disease Control and Prevention have *estimated* that each year smoking reduces the potential life span of tobacco users by five *million* life-years. This represents five *million* (5,000,000) benefit-years (a benefit-year is a continuous twelve month period in which retirement benefits would be paid by the Social Security Administration) that would be paid from the Social Security Trust Fund. Assuming that the average retiree would receive a net income of $8,400 per year, we smokers are saving the taxpayers $4,200,000,000 (that's 4.2 *billion* dollars) per year by dying off before we become social parasites. And, in addition to the savings that arise from not living long enough to drain Social Security, we smokers are also paying additional taxes that non-smokers do not have to fork over. Let's (conservatively) assume that ten million people are smoking an average of one pack of cigarettes per day, and that the total federal taxation on that pack of cigarettes is $1 per pack. A little basic mathematics and you realize that smokers are contributing $3,650,000,000 (3.65 *billion* dollars) per year in additional taxes. Take that, and then add the savings from not having to pay five million years of benefits to dead smokers, and you realize that smokers are making a positive contribution to the federal treasury to the tune of 7.85 *billion* dollars per year. Even if there were a federal tax of twenty-five cents per pound on ice cream it would require 31.4 *billion pounds* of Ben and Jerry's Cherry Garcia to have the same impact on the federal budget as us law-abiding smokers. Not only that, it would also require that every man, woman and child on the planet consume just over 5.2 pounds of ice cream every year.

The previous paragraph does not mention the obvious fact that smoking is vital to the economic health of at least two states, Kentucky and North Carolina, and is a significant contributor to the economies of several others. If tobacco consumption falls, the economies of these two states would collapse to a level currently found in places such as Botswana and North Korea. If the current incomes of tobacco farmers, their helpers, and their families were to be replaced by public assistance funds there would probably not be enough money in state tax revenues to keep these formerly productive citizens above the poverty level. There might be an offsetting gain from the income taxes on bankruptcy and divorce attorneys, but not enough to justify wrecking an entire industry.

Another benefit of smoking is that I get an almost never ending stream of people that come up to me on the street or some other public place to point out that I am "polluting the air" or participating in some other non-statutory "crime" against the "environment." What really adds a humorous tone to such accusations is that they are usually made while both the accuser and I are being enveloped a cloud of partially-burned hydrocarbons emanating from the exhaust pipes of a city bus. If I were to give off as much smoke as a city bus I would have three burning cigarettes in my mouth, one in each hand, one in each nostril and in my left ear. I would also have to run up and down Santa Monica Boulevard at thirty miles per hour while smoking like the proverbial chimney to cover as much area as a city bus. But since a city bus won't sit there and listen to a sermon from one of these tireless guardians of personal liberty, I get the pleasure of laughing hysterically at the vacant expressions on their faces when I point out that the aforementioned bus is a danger to both our well-beings. If I really want to confuse them I ask them to cite an example of a person struck and killed by a pack of cigarettes while crossing the street or when was the last time that they read of a smoker driving the wrong way on Interstate 10 causing an accident that killed a carload of innocent people.

A well-meaning but usually misinformed observer (such as the reader of this essay) might interject "Well, what about the health risks from second hand smoke?" I would first point out that the correct term is "Environmental Tobacco Smoke." That question would force me to ask if you would be able to point out a single published report in the reputable scientific literature that cites controlled clinical and/or laboratory data that can point to a single case of any disease that can be conclusively traced to second hand smoke via the established techniques of epidemiology. Allow me to save you some time by pointing out that there are no published data that will support your position. But who needs facts, especially when those nasty little facts would weaken (if not totally invalidate) your position?

Nor is such disregard for minor details like "facts" unique to the United States of America. Apparently, the people who published the following statements have reached the startling conclusion that Canadians are actually dumber than their neighbors, that group of intellectual titans commonly known as "The American Public." If you think the American taxpayers are being screwed royally, take a look at what gets published as fact in the Great Frozen North:

1. Two thirds of smoke from a cigarette is not inhaled by the smoker, but enters the air around the smoker.

Eh! We should move to the U.S. and run for President because we're too stupid to inhale. Eh?

2. Second-hand smoke has at least twice the nicotine and tar as the smoke inhaled by the smoker.

I am NOT misquoting this statement. All I want to know is, if a smoker inhales an amount of smoke containing X micrograms of tar and nicotine and some of that nicotine is absorbed by the smoker, how in the Hell you wind up with 2X micrograms of tar and nicotine in the exhaled smoke. Unless the smoker's lungs are producing the crap themselves, the above "fact" is physically impossible in that it violates the Law of Conservation of Mass.

3. Regular exposure to second-hand smoke increases the chances of contracting lung disease by 25% and heart disease by 10%.

"Regular exposure" is NOT defined.

4. Second-hand smoke aggravates symptoms in people with allergies and asthma, and can cause eye, nose and throat irritations, headaches, dizziness, nausea, coughing and wheezing in otherwise healthy people.

These symptoms can also be repeatedly induced by reading such pseudo-science as the above collection of chiropractic nonsense.

5. Children have a higher metabolism and can absorb higher amounts of smoke than adults.

Don't let children smoke! At least make them get a job and buy their own instead of stealing yours.

6. Infants and children exposed to second-hand smoke are more likely to suffer chronic respiratory illness, impaired lung function, middle ear infections, food allergies and can even succumb to sudden infant death syndrome.

Again, statements without any supporting data.

7. .4 million Canadian homes with children under 12 years of age report regular exposure to second-hand smoke.

2.4 million Canadian homes have fireplaces, burning moose meat on the stove, etc. So what?

8. Electronic air cleaning systems would need to increase the air-exchange rate a thousand fold to be effective—resulting in gale force winds!

Does that also mean that the air cleaning systems in hospitals, restaurants, and airports are ineffective too?

9. Increasing ventilation will dilute the smoke in a room, but will not make it safe since there is no known safe level of exposure to the carcinogens in cigarette smoke.

Guess what? There's no established toxic level either!

And now for this year's best example of spending the taxpayer's money to prove the obvious:

10. Canadians spend most of their time indoors.

And we thought they spent all their spare time sun bathing on the tropical beaches of Hudson Bay!

Many years ago the great American newspaper columnist H. L. Mencken wrote about the activities of a group of citizens that he called the "uplifters." To Mencken, the "uplifters" were ceaselessly attempting to save mankind from some dangerous substance, such as alcohol in the case of the Prohibitionists of his day, that could easily be controlled (so the "uplifters" claimed) if only the substance in question were to be declared illegal. I can't read his classic column "The Uplifters Try It Again" without pausing to wonder what Mencken would have thought about our latest attempt to "govern via legislative fiat" via the unofficial (but oh-so politically correct) *jihad* against the still legal substance known as tobacco. Prohibition was a dismal failure because its supporters failed to remember one simple fact about "human nature": You can't legislate morality.

Allow me to restate the circumstances surrounding the posting of "Why I Smoke":

1. It was published on a web site that emphasized humor and satire.

2. Jeremiah Wazza-Boolphrogg? Robert Blake Handgun Safety Institute? Gimme a break!

3. It ridicules people that have appointed themselves as the guardians of public health and morality.

4. The final paragraph restates the purpose of "Why I Smoke" by referring to a classic social essay by H.L. Mencken.

I received 148 e-mails responses regarding the above essay. Of these, 145 were complimentary, 2 were in a language that has resisted all attempts at translation, and 1 reply that was negative, but did serve to prove beyond any reasonable doubt that there are some people who take themselves entirely too seriously. The text of that reply is as follows:

> "You should be ashamed for promoting smoking when everyone knows that smoking is a dangerous addiction that hurts our children, damages the environment, and has driven up the cost of health care. We should be listening to our compassionate leaders like Bill and Hillary Clinton, not reactionary puppets of the tobacco industry. Only when we all understand the dangers to our planet posed by smoking, will we make any progress in stopping the plague of tobacco use."

To which I issued the following reply:

"Does the word 'satire' ring a bell?"

S/h/it did not reply. And on the outside chance that s/h/it reads this:

Congratulations, you have your fifteen minutes of fame and,in doing so; have brightened the day of no less than fifteen thousand people by demonstrating that no one has a monopoly on stupidity.

At first glance, the above may seem to be nothing more than a case of mistaken intent, such as taking Swift literally when he argues that Irish children be sold to the well-to-do English where they would be eaten. That would be understandable except that, when I reread that e-mail, I got the distinct impression that the writer belongs to a small (rephrasing, hopefully small) section of society that feels that its members are better-qualified (or divinely ordained) to make decisions than certain "not-compassionate" people (such as myself and, probably, you).

And that is one frightening thought.

I wish that I could honestly write off comments such as the ones contained in that e-mail by invoking Hanlon's Razor ("Never attribute to malice that which can be adequately explained by stupidity").

Unfortunately, I can't do that. And that is not a good thing. Not good at all.

8.

Religion in Wonderland

The only thing that stops God sending a second Flood is that the first one was useless.

Nicholas Chamfort

When I was a kid growing up in central Georgia, there was an expression that people used to describe someone who, for some reason, had renounced their previous "lives of sin" and had "accepted the Lord Jesus" or something to that effect. When this phenomenon occurred, the person in question was said to have "got religion." This was usually the result of some personal crisis such as a divorce, an accident (as in motor vehicle accident since it was very difficult to "get religion" by accident), or as a condition of probation imposed by either the courts or an irate spouse.

Regardless of the precipitating factor(s) this person would usually exhibit atypical behavior patterns such as being sober at 5:00 PM on Saturday's during football season, being home before midnight, or attending church services even if those services weren't funerals. This unusual behavior would usually subside or even disappear completely after a short period of time, but I do recall some cases that persisted for many years and I doubt if those cases will ever be completely cured. Of course, all this occurred in the pre-Internet era.

The Internet has, among other things, allowed those who wish to study all things religious to become brainwashed in the comfort of their own homes and avoid the previous inconveniences of having to live with someone else's schedule or sit through an hours-long sermon from someone with the oratorical skills of Richard Nixon. It is now possible to "convert" yourself into membership in any of dozens of faiths, sects, branches, schisms or heresies without ever having experienced the pleasure that one gets by chasing a Jehovah's Witness from your front porch at gunpoint. For those who wish to pursue this hocus-pocus as a vocation, it is also possible to earn one's credentials as a minister or some other official certification as a ringmaster in whatever faith is willing to sign on the bottom line (for an appropriate fee. of course).

As I noted above, there are about as many web pages and chat rooms devoted to religious topics as there are morons using the web. What sets this particular crowd apart is their belief that they alone are correct and everyone else is wrong, which means that this gives these keepers of the true faith the franchise from God to decide who gets into the VIP section in the afterlife. More importantly it also gives them the right to decide who gets condemned to eternity in Hell or in places like Modesto, California or Gallup, New Mexico if Hell is having one of its standing room only periods.

There are, of course, web sites that are dedicated to scholarship and serious study of a wide variety of religious topics and you can actually find quite a few sites that provide some very well researched data without getting a sermon or homily thrown in your face. These sites are usually run by academic organizations with no particular ideological ax to grind with anyone and in most cases welcome dissenting interpretations of their data as well as challenges to their conclusions regarding said data. But, I can personally assure you, such sites are in the minority when you are researching information regarding canonical scriptures used in the first century of the Christian era.

In order to fully appreciate the hypocrisy of theses "religious" chat rooms, you must have a basic understanding of the subject being debated. For those of you who did not pay attention during world history in high school or during those weekly brainwashing sessions known as Sunday School or Catechism, let me give you a brief history of Christianity.

In the Beginning...

The whole thing started with the original alternative lifestyle commune, the Garden of Eden. After Adam and Eve broke the lease by eating something that would make them too much like the landlord they were evicted and became the patron saints of the homeless. They also did a whole lot of "begatting", an archaic term for sex.

After a few pages of begatting, the landlord got really upset with the neighborhood and instituted the first urban renewal project on record by drowning everyone except for one family that had the foresight to buy a houseboat. After another round of begatting, an obscure tribe of nomads won the first Power Ball lottery and got a verbal contract from God to be the Chosen People. A few more begattings later, and after a hostile takeover attempt at Jacob, Inc. we find that the Chosen People have been chosen to be slaves in Egypt so that Moses can lead them back to where they came from so that they can smite some Philistines (the original Palestinians).

Although they were supposedly the elect of God, the Chosen People were periodically invaded and enslaved by the Assyrians, Babylonians, Persians, Greeks, and finally the Romans. It was the Romans who got the whole show rolling by taxing everything in sight, thus upsetting the high priests of the temple who felt that they alone had the power to screw the people out of their money.

Into this sorry mess stepped one Jesus of Nazareth, who promptly pissed off both sides of the money-grubbing dispute by gathering a large following and by teaching using stories that made about as much sense as a Woody Allen movie. This got Jesus a one way trip to the lethal injection chamber, but he beat the odds and wouldn't stay dead for any appreciable length of time.

After a few years of clandestine activities, Jesus' followers took over what was left of the Roman Empire and replaced it with their own little shell game. They also promptly got even with the original Chosen People for not buying into the game earlier and burned the rest at the stake.

(Do you get the impression that being the Chosen People is not exactly all its cracked up to be?)

After a few centuries of war, famine, pestilence and some unexpected competition from Arabia the Christians (as they now called themselves) seemed to be on top of their game and had the West pretty well under their control. But some guy named Luther came along and rocked the boat by saying that you don't need the middle man to get your money to God for you and thus started what was later known as "the Reformation", although nothing was really reformed.

The English got into the act because Henry VIII wanted a divorce. His loyal subjects got into the act by beheading a few of the nobility and having a nice civil war, which chased a lot of Puritans to North America and provided the plot for several Hawthorne novels. This forced relocation also killed off most of the aboriginal inhabitants of the New World, but this was acceptable since they weren't Christians anyway.

After a civil war of its own, a few world wars and an economic fiasco called the Great Depression (because of all the people that were depressed about it) somebody decided that America was really the Holy Land and that God had changed His mind about the original Chosen People, giving the title to the Americans and sending the runners-up back to Palestine to smite the descendants of the Philistines.

You might have noticed that, in the above history lesson, I neglected to mention by name any of the various denominations, sects, branches, covens, klaverns, or whatever self-identification groups the Christians seem to be so fond of dividing themselves (or consigning their enemies) into. I did this deliberately as to allow the readers to enjoy doing this themselves since this seems to be a favorite pastime among the Christians. When not praying for their own "salvation" most Christians can still be found at prayer, except they are then praying for their enemies' banishment to Hell, once they are certain that they themselves will not be sharing the same pit of flaming brimstone as that no-good sinner next door.

This brings us to the point where a closer study of some of the better known denominations would be of benefit. Please note that by "denominations" I am referring to various branches of the big olive tree known as Christianity and not to the "denominations" of the greenish pieces of paper which are placed into the collection plates at worship services, although the latter is generally worshiped with the same fervor as God and pursued with the same enthusiasm as a front row seat in Heaven.

The Roman (and Various Other Flavors) Catholic Church

In military conflicts and other such acts of diplomacy, the winner gets to write history. When it comes to the history of religion, however, the first one in line gets to not only write history but gets to invent a lot of it as well. This is best explained by observing the history of the Roman Catholic Church, the Microsoft of Christianity.

The Catholics, like Microsoft, were the first ones to identify a new and untapped market segment and both have been vigorous in protecting their market share ever since. And, since there is not a religious Federal Trade Commission, the Catholics are free to use any trick in the book to advance their agenda whereas Microsoft has to be careful not to upset the Justice Department all over again and be forced to spend a few million bucks to get off their hook before they can get back to the business of putting their own hooks into everyone else.

From a historical perspective the Roman Catholics were the first ones out of the gate and for almost a thousand years had no real competition (see Protestants in the next section). They used this period to almost completely corrupt the teachings of the man they supposedly represented by introducing enough dogmatic *caca del toro* that a believer had to rely on any number of church officials just to avoid offending God, much less the local ruling class, which was also under the control of the same set of church flunkey's.

The Roman Catholic Church is the perfect example of a self-perpetuating pyramid sales operation in that there is one guy at the top with various levels under him. These lower levels, as in a pyramid, get wider the closer you get to the bottom level until the actual church members wind up supporting everyone above them. The fact that the upper levels of the hierarchy serve no useful purpose other than to make work for themselves, which the lower levels must pay for, is not lost on the higher-ups in this scheme. The upper levels of the church are totally dedicated to keeping their jobs and making sure that no one rocks the old fishing boat.

At the top of this organization is the "Pope", who supposedly is the latest in a long of successors of the apostle Peter. This top seat only occasionally comes up for grabs on occasions when the current occupant either resigns or dies, although in the early Middle Ages being Pope was not a position you aspired to if being stabbed, smothered, or poisoned was not on your agenda. However, if you survived long enough, being the Supreme Pontiff of the Holy Roman Catholic Church was a pretty good job because you got to live in castles and be waited on hand and foot by people who were after your job. You also had the power to damn your opponents to eternal punishment in Hell if they tried too overtly to hasten your departure to your heavenly reward.

Now, not just anyone can be elected Pope. Although in theory this position belongs to the one God chooses as the most pious and most like the man whose teachings the Church is supposed to emulate, the short list for promotion is in practice limited to members of an organization called the "College of Cardinals", the "princes" of the Church. The Cardinals are the legislative body of the Church and the competition for a seat here is just as dirty as in the more secular world, if your idea of a great job happens to be covering up for priests that are child molesters, alcoholics or exhibiting some other form of social dysfunction.

To assist the Cardinals in the maintenance of order among the faithful is an army composed of "bishops" and "archbishops", more commonly known as "cardinals-in-training." These, in turn, have an even larger group of "monsignors" and "priests" that actually have to go out among the flock to make sure that everyone is giving their fair share to support this mob, freeing the higher-ups to fight among themselves for promotion to the next level in the hierarchy of heaven's servants. And to this Pharaoh's army don't forget to add the monks, brothers, nuns and seminarians (priests in training, sort of like Oliver Twist being trained by Fagan) whose sole purpose is to make the rest of the church feel guilty about not being religious enough. This brings us to the lowest level of the church, the members.

The "members" of the Catholic Church are variously known as "parishioners", "communicants" "dupes", or "suckers." They live in loosely formed groups called "parishes" and attend worship services where they take "communion", and they have been "duped" into believing that all these various rites and even more various levels of clergy are vital for their salvation, which makes them "suckers" for the next scam the Catholic Church hierarchy invents in order to either fleece the members or scare them into meek compliance. Collectively, the "civilian" (not dressed funny) members are known as the "laity" because the can get laid without attracting a production team from "60 Minutes" (as opposed to the ones in uniforms, which can't even molest a choirboy anymore without being dragged onto the 6 o'clock news). The others are referred to as "clergy", whatever that term means.

Over the centuries, there have been several branches that either split away from the Roman Church or were driven away from it by its own follies. There is the Greek Orthodox Church (which replaces the sacramental wine with Ouzo), the Russian Orthodox Church (which replaced excommunication with firing squads and the Gulag), the Armenian Orthodox Church (which replaced Hell with Turkey), and the Church of England (which replaced everything and started its own franchise).

Protestants Who Doth Protest Too Much

Once upon a time there was a man named Martin Luther who had a minor dispute with the Roman Catholic Church regarding the fund raising tactics used in those times. Since this was 500 years before the McCain-Feingold Campaign Finance Reform Act, he resorted to a more populist approach and posted his objections to the door of a cathedral in Germany because Larry King had not yet been born. The end result was eventually called either the Protestant Reformation or the Great Heresy, depending on which side you think God happens to be on.

The Protestants, as they became known, wasted no time before becoming almost as overbearing as their Catholic forefathers by adopting the same evangelism methods that had proven effective in the past such as hanging, beheading, torture, and the ever-popular burning at the stake. Although these methods met with limited success when used to convert the unbelievers, they were highly effective in assuring that the converts stayed converted.

The Protestant philosophy was embraced by the British royal family because they didn't enjoy having to share power with anyone, much less some Italian who got his job by being just as ruthless as his competitors. In fact, the English monarchs were so taken with the idea of being the head of both the Church and the State they kicked all the priests and their supervisors out of the country, confiscated church property, and began a vigorous conversion (persecution) program on anyone who was left. Oh those rare occasions when the

Catholics were able to come out of hiding because the reigning monarch was a loyal Catholic they repaid the favor, in spades, by using the same tactics as their Protestant brethren.

After a few centuries of this both sides called a truce and agreed to only persecute their own followers unless it was deemed more practical to persecute the other side for reasons to be determined on a case by case basis.

However, a few malcontents decided to head for parts unknown and sailed to North America taking with them only the most basic of creature comforts such as Bibles and guns. Upon arrival in the new Promised Land, they applied both of these meager creature comforts liberally to the aboriginal inhabitants with the same results obtained in the Old World: wars, famine, genocide, and slavery.

Unlike the Catholics (see above) or the Mormons (see below) the Protestants come in more varieties than you can count because they have all, essentially, rejected any form of central authority over their individual churches. This seemingly anarchist trend does have the advantage of keeping the proceeds from the collection plate closer to home where it can be used to further the good works of the church such as picketing, boycotting, or otherwise pestering anything or anyone that they don't agree with.

Of all the religious factions the Protestants are the most aptly named because it seems they are always protesting something or another every time you turn on the television or pick up a newspaper. The more fundamentalist congregations have, in the past, boycotted the Walt Disney company and its assorted theme parks (for being too pro-gay rights), the Coca-Cola company (same thing), and Planned Parenthood (for abortions that deprive the churches of a new generation to brainwash).

Mormon, Inc: A Religion for Real Americans!

If your tastes in religion run more along the lesser-known domestic lines, there is alternative to the high-priced imported brands. "The Church of Jesus Christ of Latter Day Saints", AKA the "Mormons", is a full-blooded home grown honest to God (in theory, at least) all-American religion, made in America, by Americans, for Americans. Although usually snubbed as a minor heresy by its older cousins it usually turns the other cheek and refuses to return the favor, at least in the public record, but saves its denunciations of the others for the privacy of its own sanctuaries.

This denomination is the creation of Joseph Smith, who first published his "Book of Mormon" in 1830. This book, which is still the subject of an intense plagiarism versus inspiration debate (as well as a debate among librarians whether to put it on the fiction or non-fiction shelf), is, at best, the first example of American science fiction. If you think that what the other groups of Christians believe is a bit far-fetched, check this one out.

Smith claimed that one night, while he was praying (something he apparently was quite fond of doing) an angel named Moroni dropped by to take him to a place where he found two plates made of gold on which were inscribed the "record" of the aboriginal inhabitants of the New World. This record, written in a language that had not been spoken in almost two thousand years, was translated into English by Smith with the help of some kind of magical sun glasses that had been provided by the angel. Once Smith had finished the translation the angel took the plates and sun glasses to Heaven, leaving Smith in charge of the "re-established" church founded by no less than Jesus Himself!

According to Mormon dogma, the original inhabitants of America were not some rag-tag bunch of Pre-Stone Age hunter/gatherers that wandered over from Asia via the Bering Land Bridge during the most recent Ice Age but were actually a rag-tag bunch of refugees from the Nation of Israel who fled something or another around 650 BC in a fleet of sailing ships (because El Al did not have direct flights at that time).

After arriving in North America these people continued their pre-exile activities of building cities, worshiping in their temples, and fighting among themselves. In fact, they were so efficient in the fighting among themselves category that they were able to erase every trace of their existence to the point that no evidence of them can be found to this day!

The Mormons have some rather, shall we say, untraditional teachings when compared to their elder cousins, the Catholics, or the other Protestant denominations. What is truly amazing is that they seem to have copied the worst administrative ideas of every other Christian group and then thrown in an obsession with worldly material success, since they believe if you are on good terms with God you will be rewarded with money in this life and a chance to become the God of your own pyramid scheme in the hereafter.

The Mormon organization has a vested interest in your success because you have to ante up ten per cent of your prosperity off the top to send in to Salt Lake City just to stay a member in good standing of God's All-American Country Club. Where he money goes from there, only God knows and since God is also a Mormon, the money trail ends there.

As I mentioned earlier in this section, the Mormons have adopted the worst habits of both the Catholics and the other Protestant denominations to make what no one but another Mormon will recognize as an organization supposedly dedicated to keeping its members off God's shit list. In the pope position they have a "prophet, seer, and revelator" who is placed in this position after a lifetime of back stabbing, political deal-making, money raising and not being caught with his hands in the cookie jar service in the administrative wing of the church. Outliving the other potential candidates is seen as a sign that God is smiling on this particular person, although a favorable ancestry is not necessarily a prerequisite.

You might think that once some elderly gentleman has risen to this prominent level that he could just kick back and maintain the status quo with a few photo-ops or other such public relations visits among the faithful. You would, of course, be wrong because God seems to have the need to fine-tune the doctrines of His church. Particularly when money is involved.

In the late 1960s the Mormons still held the pre-American Civil

War beliefs that had been "revealed" to their founder, Joseph Smith. Among these sacred teachings was one that said that, although people of African ancestry could be members of the Mormon flock, they were not allowed to hold any type of administrative positions nor were they eligible to assume any of the roles of "elder", "deacon", or anything else that would have placed them in positions of authority over the Caucasian members of the church.

This divine commandment was all well and good, until the basketball team of church-owned and directed Brigham Young University began to gain national prominence. Several of the team's potential opponents were talking openly about refusing to play a school whose parent organization held that discrimination against blacks was, in some cases, ordained by God. Since this boycott would have led to the loss of considerable radio and television revenue, not to mention casting the church in a negative light, it seemed that only a miracle could save the church from a financial and public relations disaster. And just when the faithful thought all was lost, God came to their rescue.

The "Prophet, Seer, and Revelator" made use of the latter of his titles and revealed that God had changed His mind and that now Black members had the same rights and responsibilities as the other members. The crisis was diverted by the timely divine edict from God.

The same thing happened a few years later when a wealthy church member left a sizable bequest to the church that contained another potentially embarrassing situation, this one involving a large block of common stock in the Pepsi Cola Company.

The church was faced with what appeared to be either a classic conflict of interest at best or a textbook example of hypocrisy. From the very beginnings of Mormon history, church members had been ordered to abstain from any beverage that contained caffeine. Now the church was being presented with a multi-million dollar bequest of stock in a company whose main product contained this same ingredient, caffeine. Take a wild guess at what happened next.

You guessed it. God "revealed" that He had changed his mind yet again and was really alright for the church to own a few million bucks worth of Pepsi Cola stock and it was also kosher for the faithful to drink soda pop, if it was Pepsi, naturally.

Under the "Prophet, Seer, and Revelator" there can be found an increasingly broader and broader support system until you once again wind up at the bottom of the pyramid where you find the same old song and dance routine that is fed the members, who foot the bill for everyone else. The members of the Mormon church are expected to have as many children as possible, to insure that the church will always be able to show a positive growth curve when they run out of drunks, psychopaths, addicts and other social rejects to pester until they sign on the bottom line.

But what makes the Mormons unique is their belief that, if you are a really good little Mormon, you can be the God of your own world! Since God was once a man, they reason (according to their teachings from the Moronic angel or someone) that after a suitable and varied period of time all good Mormons will get to run their own show on some other world. Whether this world will be like Earth or not is open to debate, but you would think that if you were finally elevated to this level you wouldn't be stuck as God of the Klingons or the Romulans.

Oh Brother, Where Art Thou?

One of the few positive things I have personally gotten out of web surfing in general and chat rooms in particular is the confirmation of my impression that religious tolerance is a joke in modern society. The vast majority of the deeply religious people in the real world seem to have an opinion along the line of "You are free to believe whatever you want as long as you agree with me." And in most religious chat rooms, woe be unto you if you are not some kind of lobotomized fundamentalist Christian zombie.

The Christian chat rooms seem to incorporate the worst antisocial behavior patterns from all the other rooms and then attempt to justify them on the basis of some set of principles that they alone are qualified to interpret. I wonder what the founder of this little social club would think if he sat in on a typical chat room full of people that are supposed to be his followers?

Please don't think I am about to engage in some form of Christian-bashing because I'm not. What I am about to do is shine the lamp of objective observation and let the cow chips fall where they may. I just happen to find the Christian chat rooms to be the antithesis of everything they supposedly represent; that is to say, they are anything but Christian. I merely chose the rabid fundamentalists because they are such easy targets!

Most religious chat rooms are usually divided into sections for the major world faiths and further subdivided by denomination, branch, sect, cult, age, sex and medication used on a daily basis. There are rooms for Christian teens and Catholic singles, Jewish chat and Muslim chat, Hindu chat (didn't we already disprove that?), chanting, and Wiccan divorcees taking Zoloft.

The one thing all of the religious rooms have in common is an absolute intolerance for anyone whose beliefs are contrary to the accepted party line. The party line is often spoken by an individual that I refer to as the Alpha and Omega, who must have the first and last word on all things theological. The Alpha and Omega has also taken on the role of Grand Inquisitor, lest some unenlightened heretic contaminate the room with unclean (or God forbid, logical) beliefs.

Should you want to see a real-life equivalent of the Three Stooges debating Abbot and Costello, throw any of the following four statements into a religious chat room:

1. Jesus wasn't a Christian, he was a Jew

2. Jesus wasn't white

3. Jesus didn't speak the King's English

About half of the words generally attributed to Jesus are really what someone else "wished" Jesus had said.

Any one of the above propositions is enough to cause the snake charmers to fly into a maniacal frenzy in which the Bible will be quoted extensively (in the King James version, of course). You will also told you are in danger of eternal damnation and the only way to avoid being sent to your room without your supper for all eternity is to immediately fall to your knees and beg forgiveness from a wrathful God who really loves you after all.

On those rare occasions when someone does get a question through the clamor known as a Christian chat room and this question requires more than a simple yes or no answer, the Alpha and Omega (or one of his acolytes) will intone the standard reply to any question requiring more than a third-grade education: "THE BIBLE SAYS…!" followed by reference to whatever passage, usually taken out of context, that seems to justify the position of the snake kissers down at the First Southern United Pentecostal Full Gospel Temple of the Assembly of the Chosen Few.

I am being unfair? Oh ye of little faith! After an hour in a Christian chat room Jesus himself would join the Hare Krishnas! Pick up your crosses and follow me into the sacred temples of religious chat.

The first thing you notice about religious chat rooms is that they have displaced the marketplace or the temple as "the" place to be seen praying and thus prove to everyone else what a good Christian you are. Of course since you are (hopefully) smart enough not to use your real name in a chat room of any kind, you are really only convincing yourself that you are really a true believer because no one else has the slightest idea who you are. And given the low regard that Jesus held those of his contemporaries that engaged in such behavior, you can rest assured that Jesus isn't reading their self-flattering pseudo-prayers either.

Once you enter one of these rooms you soon learn that although the Tower of Babel caused unlimited confusion in the Old

Testament, the followers of the New Testament have rebuilt it to rival its former glory. The problem of knowing which group a chatter belongs to is usually solved by using some of the following code words or abbreviations:

1. AG Assembly of God
2. LDS Latter Day Saints (Mormons)
3. CG Church of God
4. SB Southern Baptist
5. CC Church of Christ
6. PH Pentecostal Holiness

Once you have identified someone whose ideology is closest to your own, you might think that joining in the spiritual discussions would be quite easy and a source of both inspiration and comfort. Think again!

As I stated earlier, the Christian Chat rooms are probably the least friendly places you will encounter in cyberspace. For some reason the Christians that have chosen to wander in this wilderness are not exactly what you would imagine they would be. Take a look at this little snippet of chat.

lds_kid_on_mission: any LDS people in here?

me: hello room

jesus_loves_me: THIS IS A CHRISTIAN ROOM!!!!!

avenging angel: get lost you stinking mormon

jesus_loves_me: WE BELIEVE IN THE BIBLE HERE!!!!!!

this_jew_is_4_jesus: Jesus was called Rabbi, that makes him a jew not a christian

assembly_of_god_rules: if you aren't AG you not a Christian

avenging_angel: screw the AGs, they suck!

jesus_loves-me: JESUS WAS A CHRISTIAN YOU JEW LIAR AND CHRIST KILLER!!!!

jesus_loves_me: THE AG IS THE ONLY CHRISTIAN CHURCH!!!!!

me: goodbye room

And so on and so on until even God has enough of this garbage and causes a server shutdown.

The rudeness, stupidity, and the general abandonment of anything close to rational thought are just as present in the chat rooms that God's latest crop of self-appointed prophets have appropriated for their pulpits as they are anywhere else in chat. And, as you have probably guessed, the (alleged) religious chat rooms have their own set of externally-derived rules, just like the other rooms.

The Wilcox-McCandlish Law of Online Discourse Evolution, developed by Bryce Wilcox and Stanton McCandlish back in the remote USENET days, is perhaps the most seminal statement describing the nature of chat room conversation (and, one of the most applicable to religious chat rooms). Paraphrased, this famous law states:

The chance of success of any attempt to change the topic or direction of a discussion (D) in a chat room is directly proportional to the quality (Q) of the current content.

Or, in mathematical terms,

$$D = 1/Q \times 100$$

The above observation is expanded in McCandlish's Third Corollary to the Wilcox-McCandlish Law, which I will paraphrase as:

> Any attempt at recourse to formal logic or identification of classic fallacies within a [religious] chat room will automatically increase the irrationality of the discussion already in progress.

Since religious chat is one of those places where everyone claims to be speaking on God's behalf and is therefore invariably correct, leads to the necessity of Danth's Law of Internet debating, which is recognized as a truism throughout the Internet. This law states that:

> "If someone announces that they've won an Internet forum discussion, they haven't."

This law is said to be named after a forum poster known as "danth", who declared victory in an argument he had already lost in the eyes of most observers. It is not recorded if "danth" had violated

Friedman's Corollary.

Unfortunately, you do not have to be in a religious chat room to be exposed to someone that is convinced that you need to hear the Gospel. Periodically, some of the Christian chatters slip past the guards and head for the other rooms where they annoy the other chatters until either the others send them to Iggy-world or the Apostle to the Gentiles wanna-be gets tired of trying to be heard over the usual din of country music and brainless gibberish the non-religious chatters are forced to endure on a daily basis.

For those who are always looking for new ways to amuse themselves in chat rooms, I would like to suggest a game that I call "Pin the Tail on the Jackass." In this game, any idiot who wants to preach their version of the Gospel is automatically chosen as the 'Jackass" and the various chatters try to "Pin" the "Tail" of logical or non-dogmatic reasoning, smart remarks, or general abuse on the previously-identified "Jackass."

A brief example of this game might read as follows:

john_3_16: hello room

aussie_with_an_attitude: what's up john?

me: got any scotch john?

john_3_16: I have good news! Jesus loves you!

metz_fan: thought Jesus got traded to the dodgers

too_kool_4_u_bitch: who the f__k is Jesus?

me: does Jesus have any scotch?

aussie_with_an_attitude: feed Jesus to the wombats, mate

john_3_16: Jesus wants to love you too

metz_fan: queer corner is down the hall

too_kool_4_u_bitch: hey, I'm not busy! Does Jesus cyber?

john_3_16: Jesus is coming soon!

me: Jesus takes Viagra?

aussie_with_an_attitude: damn, don't need the wombats getting any hornier than they are! 86 the idea of feeding the spick to the wombats!

metz_fan: trade Jesus 2 tickets to the cubs' game for some Viagra!

too_kool_4_u_bitch: wooooohooo, get me Jesus on the line!

Feel free to modify this game and make up your own rules as you play along, since the Jesus-pimps have such a limited outlet for fun that anything has to be better than that manifestation of intellectual atrophy known as "witnessing."

Buckle Your Seat Belts, You Won't Believe This!

After reading all the above, the following will undoubtedly cause a lot of a people to sit back and say, "What in the Hell is he doing now?" In this section I will do my best to alienate those that I might have missed earlier in the essay by coming to the defense of the good Christians of both the Internet and the real world. I do this because I have always thought that if you want to play the game you play by the same set of rules, across the board, no exceptions and no favorites.

Unfortunately it seems that a lot of people and various organizations feel that they are above the rules as long as it involves "Christian-bashing."

It seems that not a week goes by without someone, somewhere, going into court with a lawsuit which alleges that some apparently innocent behavior must be proscribed because it is a violation of the First Amendment to the Constitution in that it "violates" the "establishment clause", which says that there will be no "official" United States religion which will be supported by forced donations or forced participation of the citizens.

Unless you have been living in a cave in Afghanistan or a fenced-in compound in Idaho and getting your news fed to you by some "mullah", "minister", "Grand Dragon" or some other variety of control freak you are aware that there is a trend which is variously known as "transcultural learning", "religious tolerance", "non-traditional beliefs" or, by a more recognizable term, "politically correct bullshit" which seems to use this "church and state" argument as a tool to force whatever agenda that the members of this movement happen to be pushing into the public (taxpayer financed) agenda. As long as it doesn't involve anything that might be even remotely related to Christianity.

Now, My question is this: What makes the Christians such a fair target for those who scream "separation of church and state" when its a Christian matter before the bench and yet its perfectly fine if other faiths, or religions, or whatever else want the government to force "their" own beliefs down your throat using the full force of the judiciary to damn well make you listen or participate in what "they" feel is important, even if their beliefs are totally contrary to your own?

For those of you who don't remember what the First Amendment says, he it is again so you can verify that I am not misquoting anything:

> Congress shall make no law respecting an establishment of religion, or prohibiting the free exercise thereof; or abridging the freedom of speech, or of the press; or the

> right of the people peaceably to assemble, and to petition the government for a redress of grievances.

Please observe what the original document said: "Congress shall make no law respecting an establishment of religion, or prohibiting the free exercise thereof..." Now what is so controversial about that? The Bill of Rights says that Congress cannot make a law that sets up a state-sponsored church. Remember the problems that the Church of England caused among the Roman Catholics and the Protestants? If you don't, just head on over to Northern Ireland where they're still hotly debating the issue after over 300 years. The people who wrote the Constitution remembered what happens when government tries to legislate morality and they wanted to make sure that no future Congress, or President, tried to sneak in their ideas on what is kosher and what isn't. No one in their right mind would want the Pandora's Box of troubles that a state religion opens once it becomes incorporated into the law of the land!

The fact is we would all be a lot better off if the quill had run dry after the first five words, which would have saved us the trouble of dealing with (and subsequently repealing) Prohibition, the Internal Revenue Service and explaining to 18 year old why they are old enough to vote but not after having a few beers while chatting with the candidates. But it didn't and we are stuck with the American Crying Lawyers Union (ACLU) and its legions of legal vultures scurrying around the country looking for anything that can be litigated to generate tons of money for the starving lawyers of the world.

Look people, it's like this! You want to outlaw all forms of religious expression in public places, go ahead and try! Because, like cockroaches, you'll never get them all and the only thing you will accomplish is the wasting of the court's time and the taxpayer's money.

And all you people that want to shove your beliefs down someone else's throat, get real! Don't try to convert me by co-opting governmental authority to do your dirty work because if you can't show me the value of your faith in your daily lives, you are only kidding yourselves. Or maybe God.

But be careful because, from what I can read, God doesn't suffer fools lightly.

9.

How to Start Your Own Religion: A Guide for Potential Messiahs and Those that Just Want to Screw the IRS

If you are in the same boat as me you get tired of the yearly ritual of sending lots of money that you really need and don't have to the Internal Revenue Service (IRS), which has all the money it needs but still wants all of yours. After consulting every legal and semi-legal technique to make the transition from "screwed" to "screwer" I came to the conclusion that starting your own religion was the way to go. There are numerous potential benefits to starting your own religion, such as:

1. The general public is already accustomed to being screwed by organized religious groups. When you stop consider the fact that the average citizen will believe that anything they see on television is true, you will be amazed how easy it is to start your own scam. This fact alone will save you from having to create anything even remotely believable to anyone with more than a public school education.

2. The Feds hate to be accused of religious persecution, even if it's not an election year. If the Bush administration wants "faith-based initiatives" give them one! Do not, however, maintain two sets of accounting records because the second set can always be used as evidence.

3. There are already lots of people pulling the same scam, making your particular scam harder to detect. Your competition will rush to your defense if you happen to be hauled before the local Pontius Pilate because they are afraid they might be next.

4. You might accidentally get it right, which will not only make you too public a figure to mess with, but you can then earn millions of tax-free dollars by franchising the whole operation.

It makes it a lot easier to get laid on a regular basis.

Think about it! No matter where you go in the world there is already some form of religion in place, with a seemingly limitless number of religious zealots scurrying around making sure everyone is paying for whatever form of eternal bliss which sells in that particular location. Even the Communists weren't so dumb as to miss the potential for creating their own Supreme Beings. They just replaced the idea of an all-powerful being that you can't see, but want to please anyway, with an all-powerful being that you could see and had damned well better want to please if you wanted to stay alive longer than fifteen minutes. I just can't imagine Michelangelo painting a picture of Fidel Castro on the ceiling of the Sistine Chapel.

Another thing you can learn from this is that no matter how ridiculous you make the core beliefs of your new religion, you will always have a market in the population that doesn't believe a word that the government tells them. So if the local constabulary objects to your all-night "love celebrations" you can rest assured that their objections will be viewed with skepticism. You might run into some resistance from White Supremacists in Montana or the Nation of Islam in Brooklyn, but never underestimate the power of a good advertising campaign. Or the power of a good attorney.

As an example, look at what a second-rate science fiction writer named L. Ron Hubbard was able to pull off. He created his own religion, "Dianetics", after telling everyone in sight that he could take a bunch of totally illogical statements and convince the public that he had discovered the One True Faith. Now you can't watch a late night B-grade movie without being bombarded with ads promoting this scam. And to top it all, he's even dead and people are still buying into this pack of lies! If you play your cards right, you too can have the high honor of postmortem reputation enhancement.

Although it got a lot of bad press, particularly in the liberally-oriented media in the last election, the Constitution is your friend! It specifically states something to the effect that government can't go around deciding what is and what isn't religion. This means that once you have come up with your basic beliefs, they can't touch you! In fact, they will send lawyers to fight for you in case the locals don't see it your way. This may come in very handy if your core beliefs involve using what some erroneously call "illegal" drugs or having sex with people under the age of consent.

Although you may feel threatened by all the competition at first, view your competitors as learning resources. Take their good points and enhance them and replace their prohibitions with edicts that allow your new followers to keep doing what they are already doing in secret. Even better yet, sell special dispensations or waivers to those who can afford them. This will solidify your appeal with the wealthy as well as encourage the less fortunate members of your church to work harder. If some one complains about this practice, quiet them down quickly by whatever means necessary. Remember, it only took one German monk to really make a shamble of a good business plan.

All the competing ideas mean only one thing: no one has it right yet and there is always the chance that, through a lucky guess, you'll be the one to get it right and thus receive all the credit for revealing the ultimate truth to a misguided world. It's like playing the lottery, sooner or later someone has to get lucky. This will also allow you to kill off any competition while claiming divine authority for doing so.

And as for the final benefit, did you ever see a televangelist that was laying an ugly broad? If you ignore Jimmy Swaggert, who couldn't get laid in a Saigon whorehouse with an American Express Platinum card, these guys sleep with some fine babes.

As you can see, with the right plan, starting your own religion can be both a personally and a financially rewarding endeavor. The next sections deal with the "wheat and chaff" of establishing your own personal religion.

The Basics

The one thing that all commercially successful religions have in common, other than a central figure, is that they all have at least one "holy book" or set of guiding principles. Unfortunately, this has invariably led to a lot of second-guessing among the faithful as to what these teachings really mean. Be reasonable here, not even God could provide a law for every possible instance that might arise during the course of the day or whatever other time frame you use. For example, take the following simple commandment:

Thou shalt not kill.

Now that seems pretty self-explanatory, doesn't it. "You will not kill." Period. End of statement. But somebody, somewhere, had to bend the rules just enough to suit the current situation until we wound up with a commandment that had a whole pile of qualifying conditions such as:

> 1. Unless it is during an act of war, peacekeeping effort, United Nations-mandated disarmament action or for some other such noble purpose.
>
> 2. Unless in retribution for some crime against society, such as killing without divine orders or in the heat of passion.
>
> 3. Unless the son of a bitch needed killing.
>
> 4. Unless you are ordered to kill by a five hundred-year-old dog that speaks to you through a hole in the wall.

When starting your religion be sure to make you core beliefs very simple and unambiguous, since this will save your followers a lot of trouble deciding what you really meant.

If you are not of a literary bent, there are several excellent books already available that would make acceptable "Good Books." Among these, I recommend:

> *Republican Party Reptile* or *Parliament of Whores*, by P.J. O'Rourke
>
> *Generation of Swine* or *Fear and Loathing in Las Vegas*, by Hunter Thompson
>
> Anything by H.L. Mencken, but especially *A Treatise on the Gods.*

Should none of the above suggestions seem appropriate, I have included a sample chapter that should help you develop a comprehensive scared scripture, particularly if your followers are cable television addicts.

The First Book of the Stooghe, known as The Book of

Genitals

Chapter I

1. We are the Stooghe, and the story of our people begins in the Land of the First Home.

2. Where the Land of the First Home is, or what became of it, is not remembered by any living Stooghe.

3. But, yea verily, it must have existed, for we know that nothing can exist if it has not existed before.

4. The Great Stooghe, the First High God, the all-powerful Moh, ruled over His children, the Little Stooghe, and gave unto them a home in a wonderful garden where there three of every king of animal, and three suns lit the day.

5. All was good, because the Little Stooghes obeyed the Law of Moh, who, in His way, loved the Stooghe and called them His children.

6. But Moh was not happy, for there was none that He could call His equal.

7. And He spake unto His Moh-ness self, saying: I shall make another of My glorious Self.

8. And will give unto Him rule over all that I have made, as long as He knoweth His place.

9. So the Great Moh made another as Himself, and called the new god Lharrie.

10. And it came to pass that the Great Moh called the Little Stooghes together, in one place, and spake unto them, saying:

11. "Behold! I give unto you, My children, the Almost as Great Lharrie. Honor Him, and ye also honor Me.

12. "Keep ye My suggestions, (for there were not yet commandments), and all will be well.

13. "But eat ye not from the Three Trees of Life, nor make for yourselves any food from its fruit, nor smoke ye its leaves."

14. And the Little Stooghe praised Him, saying "You da man, Great Moh!" and "Left On, your Moh-ness (for the right had not been created then)."

15. And the Great Moh sat the Almost as Great Lharrie before the Little Stooghes, and gave Him dominion over them.

Chapter II

1. And all was good, until some of the Stooghe became proud and filled with vanity. They ate from the fruit of the Three Trees of Life, and smoked its leaves. They then formed themselves into a nation, and worshiped the new God, the Almost as Great Lharrie.

2. The Great Moh was enraged at this, and He called forth that all the Stooghe should come together to stand before Him, to hear His mighty words.

3. When the Stooghe were all in one place the Great Moh called the Almost as Great Lharrie to stand before Him, and spake unto Him saying,

4. "You have insulted Me, and you have caused the Stooghe to turn against Me!"

5. And then the Great Moh smote Lharrie upon His head, and across His face. He pulled forth Lharrie's tongue from His mouth, and The Great Moh smote Lharrie's eyes with His mighty fingers.

6. Then the Great Moh cast Lharrie and the Stooghe that followed Him out of the Land of the First Home, and they traveled thence to

the Land of the Second Home and called it Burbank.

7. And as it was with the Great Moh in the Land of the First Home, soon Lharrie grew tired and lonely and He made another such as Himself, and called the new god Schemp.

8. But as it had been in the Land of the First Home, some of the Stooghe loved Schemp more than they loved Lharrie.

9. So the Almost as Great Lharrie called the Almost Not Quite as Great Schemp and His followers together, where He smote Schemp in the same manner that the Great Moh had first smitten Him, and cast them out of the Land of the Second Home.

10. And they traveled to the Land of the Third Home, and the Stooghe named Bakersfield.

11. And all was again well with the Stooghe.

Chapter III

1. But the Stooghe of the Third Home and the Stooghe of the Second Home grew lonely and longed to rejoin with the Stooghe of the First Home.

2. The gods Schemp and Lharrie heard their moaning and misery and ordered that the greatest of the Stooghe of the Second and Third Worlds be found, so that he could lead the Stooghe back to the Land of the First Home to make peace with the Great Moh.

3. A great contest was held, with Stooghe from far and wide hoping to be chosen for this great honor.

4. First the Stooghe smote each other in the sacred manner that Moh had smote Lharrie, and which Lharrie had then smote Schemp.

5. Then all the pies that could be found in both the Second and Third Homes were brought out, and hurled among the Stooghe.

6. Then, at sundown, the last Stooghe who remained upright, the hero Khurley, was called forth, and the gods Lharrie and Schemp smote Khurley as they had Themselves been smitten, and then They gave unto Khurley the sacred command, SPREAD OUT!.

7. With a mighty cry of "Whooop whooop whooop....nayah nayah nayah" the hero Khurley called the Stooghe together, and led

them forth on their great journey.

8. And all was well with the Stooghe.

Chapter IV

1. The Great Moh became worried after seeing the approaching great horde of Stooghe from His temple on Mount Pasadena and said to His Glorious Self "Damn! Where did all those Stooghe come from?"

2. So He mixed the stars in the sky and caused all signs marking the roads to be changed, which deceived Khurley and caused Him to lead the Stooghe not to the First Home, but to the arid land of Barstow where some of the Stooghe said,

3. "We will stay here and dwell in the town of Laughlin."

4. Others said "We will stay here, and dwell in the town of Kingman."

5. And lo, Khurley's heart was saddened, but once again he led the Stooghe down the path to the Land of the First Home.

6. But Moh was still afraid of the great band of Stooghe that approached from the east, and He sent another plague to poison the food that sustained the Stooghe.

7. And the great oasis known as Del Taco no longer fed Khurley and the Stooghe.

8. But the gods Lharrie and Schemp heard the cry of the Stooghe, and sent down another great oasis, which was marked with the sign of arches of gold.

9. This oasis grew with each visit by the Stooghe and soon there was an oasis on every road and path.

10. And soon the Stooghe found the right path, and the Great Moh realized that He must send forth the greatest plague which He could command.

11. So He called forth the furious Harpy Courtney of Love from the Island of Gilligan and set her before the Stooghe, where she shrieked at them and made loud noises with her magic lyre.

12. But the brave band of Stooghes, having heard Khurley sing

the sacred hymn "Inna Gadda Da Vida" for years turned a deaf ear and traveled on.

13. And soon the Stooghe became a great nation, and they made unto themselves a set of laws to rule them.

14. To govern themselves they made a compact that said they would, from time to time, select the greatest Stooghes from their midst and give them great power to make even more laws which applied to all Stooghes, save the band of greatest Stooghes themselves.

15. And all was well in the land of *Stooghe.*

Once you have chosen your sacred scriptures, it is then time to lay out the ground rules that your followers must adhere to in order to stay in your (and thus God's) good graces. Most religions have some brief codification such as the Judeo-Christian "Ten Commandments." However vague and inconsistent these may be, they do represent a good starting point, if we make these commandments more consistent with our own philosophical leanings. It will also be a definite plus if you state them in a more contemporary dialect. For example:

The Nine Suggestions

Don't put your faith in no other God but me, lest I kick yo punk ass to the curb.

Don't be eye-ballin' you homey's crib, his bitch, or his ride.

No cheatin' on yo' main squeeze.

IV Kick back on that seventh day, and keep it clean for baseball and football games.

V. Don't be doin' no drivebys and offin' you homies, no matter what colors they be wearing.

VI. Don't dis you momma, or you daddy either, if you know who he be.

Don't be respectin' some jive-ass idols, or none of that Chink shit, either.

Don't be makin' up no lies about nothing, no matter what the plea-deal says.

Don't be usin' The Boss-Man's name in no trash talk.

Note that there are only nine "suggestions." This will prevent any problems with copyright infringement and will also demonstrate your unique message.

The two examples given above, "The Book of Stooges" and the "Nine Suggestions," illustrate two very important concepts regarding your new One True Faith. Any religion having a large number of rabidly-loyal followers is both totally unbelievable in its origin myth and vague in its central dogma. These concepts are so vital that they deserve detailed explanations.

Let's be honest (between ourselves) about "The Book of Stooges." No one in their right mind is going to believe it! At first glance, this might seem to be a major stumbling block. But it ceases to be a problem once you consider some of the far-fetched ideas that millions of people already accept without a second thought:

Judaism - God once made a deal with an obscure migrant shepherd (Abraham) and promised that, in return for his family's worship, He would make that family into a mighty nation (Israel).

But the ink had barely dried on the parchment before the Children of Israel wound up spending a few generations as slaves in Egypt before God got back into the act and gave them Moses to bail them out. After wandering around in the desert for 40 years they finally made it back "home" and have spent the last 3,000 years alternating between being the victor and the vanquished, with considerably more marks in the latter than in the former category, although their won-loss record is perfect since 1948 when dealing with Islamic armies (see below), a fact that Muslims would simply like to forget.

Islam - God (Al-lah) had been waiting to see if humanity would get it right, but finally gave up and sent an angel to put the word on a semi-literate caravan boss named Mohammad. Being unable to read and write, Mohammad memorized everything and started preaching to anyone that would listen. After Mohammad died a few of his followers finally got around to writing everything down, although not all True Believers agree on exactly what God meant. To prevent undue speculation and theorizing among the faithful, God has decided that all true Muslims should wage *jihad* (holy war) in perpetuity on the Jews (see above) and the Christians (see below).

Christianity - This is the group that will give you the most static about your plans to reveal the True Faith to the world, because they think that they have the Heaven and Hell franchise all to themselves and have been known to use extreme tactics to edge out the competition. But when you take a look at what they themselves believe, anything that you come up with will be just as believable, if not more so.

This is the crowd that believes, without batting an eye, and expects you to also believe:

1. That a Jewish carpenter (Jesus of Nazareth) was simultaneously human and a direct descendent of God, and made numerous statements to that effect.

2. That Jesus of Nazareth was executed because he pissed off the local religious-industrial complex. (Note: The Romans had a monopoly on the military-industrial complex at the time).

3. That Jesus was dead and buried for 3 days before coming back to life and then, after having lunch with a few friends, walked 20 miles in a single afternoon so he could go fishing with his old gang.

4. That Jesus appointed one of his fishing buddies, Simon Peter, to run things on Earth while Jesus took care of the eternity side of the business plan.

5. That anyone who does not believe all this is a Godless heathen at best, and probably a Satan-worshiping secular humanist, which places them into the same theological free-fire zone as the Jews and the Muslims (see above).

Now I ask you, given the sets of wild ideas listed above, is there anything in "The Book of Stooges" that is less rational than what members of the "Big Three" already accept?

You could use a variation of this analysis to defend your "Nine Suggestions."

1. The "Ten Suggestions" are merely a restatement of what everyone is supposed to believe anyway. But,

2. There seems to be little evidence, based on events in the world around us, that anyone makes even the feeblest attempt to incorporate similar beliefs into their own lives. Therefore,

3. So what?

Now that we have the dogma established, its time to look at how to market your new religion to the public.

Go Ye Therefore And Teach All Nations...

In order to be a successful True Light of the World you must have five things that will demonstrate the righteousness of your mission here on Earth. These are:

1. An impressive title for yourself

2. A group of hard-core, no-questions-asked followers

3. A message that people want to hear

4. A lawyer

5. A few guns, legally purchased and registered

6. Money, which will guarantee that you will always have plenty of numbers 3 and 4, above.

Each of these is so important that they must be examined in detail.

An Impressive Title

Once you have taken care of the basics, it will be time for you to give yourself a title that will impress the masses. Some titles are so popular (like "Reverend" or "Minister" or "Grand Dragon") that, if you adopt one of them, no one will think that your new religion is anything all that special or important. Since there are about as many titles as there are scams currently in operation around the world, try to call yourself something that will be easy to remember while at the same time relaying to the world your newly-created importance. Such titles that will accomplish this include:

1. True Light of the World

2. Giver of Truth and Wisdom

3. God's Other Son

Some names, however, have either already been claimed by others or carry a negative public relations theme. You should try to avoid calling yourself names such as:

1. *Ayatollah*

2. Grand Inquisitor

3. Ming the Merciless

4. *Der Fürher*

Your Followers

It is a proven historical fact that no great religious movement has been successful without a dedicated group of fanatical zealots at its core. And, surprisingly, you don't have to pick the cream of the crop from some Ivy League university to build an effective cadre of initial followers. As a historical example, consider the twelve that Jesus of Nazareth selected as his first group.

Matthew was a tax collector (and probably kept the group's books as a sideline responsibility). All the rest, with one important exception, were fisherman, a vocation not known for its high intellectual requirements. Yet inside of three years they became the base upon which one of the greatest pyramid schemes of history was built. That accounts for eleven of the twelve and leads us to look at the weakest link in the chain, Judas Iscariot.

Judas has traditionally been thought of as more "politically active" than the others, and some have gone as far as to portray him as a "freedom fighter" since "terrorist" is not a term usually associated with Biblical characters. We should give him the benefit of doubt and think of him as the type of person that, were he alive today, would probably vote for Ross Perot. Regardless of his political leanings, Judas is the one guy that almost derailed the Gospel Train before it could get out of the station.

I mention Judas because people that think along the same lines are not the type people that you want around during the period that you are developing your particular version of the True Faith, simply because they have the nasty habit of thinking for themselves and are thus not going to buy into something simply because you claim to be God's anointed prophet. People like this ask too many questions, which is something that should be discouraged among your first group of followers.

Your Message

After getting your first group of followers to sign up, the second most important thing is what you, and they, are going to say to other potential recruits. This is your message.

When deciding on a message that you will claim was given to you by God, or some other historically noteworthy personage, it is vital that you avoid telling the blundering herd of potential followers anything that they *don't* want to hear. The dominant religions are full of things that you can't do, or at least things that you shouldn't get caught doing. And believe me, no one is going to listen to you if all you have to offer is another set of no-no's.

Another tactic to avoid is the "if you can't persuade them with goodness then scare the shit out of them" philosophy of conversion to another faith. This technique, although effective in the past, has lost most of its punch simply because there is too much competition in the free market. Don't like what one group says? No problem! Just shop around until you find a faith that either lets you do what you want or has a plan available that you can participate in to avoid eternal damnation.

Instead, you should have a message that says "I, and by extension God, don't care what you do as long as you stay a dues-paying member of the spiritual country club." This will endear you to that very large segment of the population that has to sneak around doing what some of your competitors have declared "a sin." Once people learn that you aren't preaching a new line of prohibitions, and that they can raise all the Hell they want without having to worry about spending eternity there, you will have to fight off converts with a stick!

A potential source of worry is the possibility that the competition, when they realize they're losing members, might be tempted to adopt some of your "progressive" moral attitudes. Given the historical tendency of organized religions to fight tooth and nail against adopting new ideas, this is unlikely to happen fast enough to cause you to loose any sleep over the matter.

Lawyers

No matter how badly you despise the legal profession, you might as well accept one basic idea now and get it out of the way: You will need at least one lawyer, and preferably a good one. In addition to helping you avoid rendering unto Caesar any more than is absolutely necessary every April 15th; lawyers will also help you avoid becoming a martyr of the True Faith.

Martyrdom must be avoided for several reasons, with the most important one being that it would be insane to go through all the trouble of becoming the True Light of the World just to get yourself taken out of the picture by some ungrateful son of a bitch that wants your job. A good lawyer can set up a "no competition" clause in the contracts of your inner circle that will prevent them from stealing your ideas in order to set themselves up in competition against you.

If you have any reservations about lawyers, remember this. If Jesus had hired a lawyer to argue his case on that Friday morning he probably would have been sentenced to community service rather than the cross.

Guns

Guns and religion have a long history together and, in fact, most religions that are successful owe their success to guns simply because no one has ever surrendered after being threatened with Torahs, Bibles, Korans, statutes of Buddha, or copies of the Book of Mormon. When used properly, guns have always been noted for their effectiveness in converting large numbers of people to the True Faith with a minimum of effort.

Consider the success of Christianity in the New World versus the Old World. It took Christianity almost one thousand years to dominate the old Roman Empire because the technological sophistication of that remote era was, to put it mildly, a joke. Not only did Christianity have to convert each person individually it also required that an entire level of priests, bishops and other non-revenue producing employees be hired to make sure that everyone stayed converted. This, of course, occurred before firearms entered the picture.

When the Europeans entered the New World in search of whatever they were looking for, they brought along Bibles, priests, and guns. When it is remembered that the original inhabitants of the New World couldn't read and that the priests did not speak in a language that could be understood, you begin to see how effective guns were in matters spiritual. If you were offered a choice between the pre-invasion natural theology and Christianity at gunpoint, which would you choose?

You should always keep in mind that, in all probability, every potential competitor of yours will be armed to the teeth and waiting for you to do or say something that they can use to justify blasting you from here to the Ferigni home world.

Always remember that, in addition to beating a full house, a Smith and Wesson can be a highly effective tool when it comes to insuring religious orthodoxy among the faithful.

and Money

Forget that idea that money is the root of all evil because there are thousands of ways that poverty is one hell of a lot more evil than having a big pile of money. Look at it this way. Have you ever seen a television preacher that wasn't wearing a Rolex and dressed in a $2500 Brooks Brothers suit? Of course not! And have you ever seen one of these creatures when he or she or whatever wasn't begging for more money to finance this month's scam? Of course not, again! And guess what? There are scores of people that will send in their last pennies to these clowns, and do it time and time again!

You will note that you never see one of these over-dressed snake oil salesmen spending their own money. They have learned that the road to prosperity is paved with one of the most precious substances known to mankind: other people's money. Never, if at all possible, dip into your church's treasury if there is a way to let your members foot the bill. And should anyone question your fondness for wealth, remind them of what Margaret Thatcher once said, "No one would remember the Good Samaritan if he only had good intentions. He had money as well."

Then...

Now that you have the preliminaries out of the way, all that remains is to take your One True Faith to those that really need it: the rest of the civilized world. And this is where you have a big advantage over your established competition.

Prior to the Industrial Revolution (when the central figures of the other religions lived), in order to get the message to the masses you had to either:

1. Walk

2. Ride a horse, donkey, mule, camel, or some other foul-smelling, foul-tempered, semi-domesticated animal.

The invention of the printing press made things a little easier but, since not that many people could read, books weren't really that effective until a few hundred years later. Buy you, you lucky bastard, live in the Electronic Age and have the power of technology to work with.

Martin Luther had to nail a copy of his 95 Theses to s church door to get them noticed. You have both direct mail and e-mail at your disposal. It took almost forty years for the Protestant Reformation to spread across Europe. Thanks to cable television, you can promote your latest schemes all over the globe in about four seconds.

Want to inspire your widely dispersed followers in person rather than by television? Hop on your own church-sponsored private jet and to Hell with boats! (Remember the story about Jonah and the whale)?

Need to pass the collection plate? Set up a web site that allows the faithful to give up their tithes and offerings directly to your bank accounts. Not only is this cheaper and less labor-intensive than the old method, it lessens the chances that some of your "partners in the Lord's work" will be taking a few dollars off the top before sending the loot to the home office.

Technology is your friend! Treat it as you would any of friends: milk it for all that it's worth.

Wrapping It Up

In order to help you keep track of what it takes to succeed in the modern-day messiah business, I have developed a program which I have named the BULLSHIT method of religious organization. BULLSHIT is an acronym that will help you keep the program in your memory and stands for:

Build a solid organization of fanatically loyal followers. (Look at what Jim Jones was able to pull off).

Undermine your competitor's market position by any legal means necessary (or illegal, if the methods can't be traced back to you personally).

Lead from the rear (let someone else take the bullet whenever possible).

Lean on the competition (don't buy into the "What would Jesus do?" mindset. Think "What would Tony Soprano do?" instead).

Scream "religious freedom" every time you screw up and invite unwanted attention from any agency that has the authority to throw you into the slammer.

Hide behind the wall separating church and state (see the preceding statement).

Income tax can be avoided as long as you are a "non-profit corporation."

Take no prisoners.

10.

Book Review: *The Psychology of Cyber-Space*

By
John Suler, Ph.D.
Department of Psychology
Rider University

Available online at:
"http://www.rider.edu/~suler/psycyber/psycyber.html"

When I began writing this book I can distinctly remember thinking to myself that it will only be a matter of time before that realm of the human imagination known as cyber-space finds itself subjected to a critical examination under the harsh (but hopefully impartial) light of academic scrutiny. Dr. John Suler, a full professor (as opposed to the much more commonly encountered only partially full of themselves professor) at Rider University, has undertaken this dangerous journey into that fantasy land inhabited by some of the more unstable minds on this or any other known world and has emerged, seemingly unscathed, to share with the reader his learned analysis.

It is most appropriate that he has elected to publish this book via the Internet, where it has the potential to reach the millions of readers that have been reduced to functioning as mere organic input devices of their personal computers.

Dr. Suler's book, in all honesty, is a noteworthy accomplishment when you pause to consider the median intellectual capacity of the majority of the people that comprise his subject matter which, in my personal experiences online, seems to be slightly above that of a swarm of houseflies.

The first chapters of this book are devoted to defining the issues to be addressed in this study, as well as presenting a broad definition of interpersonal relations as they are manifested via the Internet. This is quite an accomplishment because, until now, the English language was thought to lack the proper words to adequately describe the disembodied citizens of the "global village." But Dr. Suler has managed to do this, although he also gives new meaning to the word "under statement" while doing so.

Consider, if you will, the first line of the first chapter, in which he notes that:

"The virtual world is quite different than the in-person world."

This statement is equivalent to stating that the grassy plains of Kenya are quite different from those seen in *The Lion King*. And this is this but one of such statements one will encounter in the paperless pages of this book. Others are less sublime, such as these observations, taken from Chapter 2, "The Psychology of the Individual in Cyber-space," in which Dr. Suler describes what he has identified as the "Online Disinhibition Effect."

> "It's well known that people say and do things in cyberspace that they wouldn't ordinarily say or do in the face-to-face world. They loosen up, feel more uninhibited, express themselves more openly...

> [They] reveal secret emotions, fears, wishes. Or they show unusual acts of kindness and generosity. We may call this 'benign disinhibition.'
>
> "On the other hand, the disinhibition effect may not be so benign. Out spills rude language and harsh criticisms, anger, hatred, even threats. Or people explore the dark underworld of the Internet, places of pornography and violence, places they would never visit in the real world. We might call this 'toxic disinhibition.'"

Here again Dr. Suler demonstrates his remarkable talent at making an understatement. This observation has been made so many times, by so many different people, from so many different backgrounds, that it should become a codicil to the Ten Commandments! Of course many people exhibit different personalities in the online world that they would never show in the real world. If your greatest unfulfilled sexual fantasy was to be trussed up in rope while being beaten by a dwarf that looks like Richard Nixon, would you bring up the subject at the after-church ice cream social? Do you want your neighbors and coworkers to know that you are a closet Nazi? A latent mass murderer? Or, God forbid, that you agree with everything Maureen Dowd and Molly Ivans ever wrote and that you voted for Ralph Nader? Of course not, unless you are attempting to use mental incompetence as a reason to apply for permanent disability from the Social Security Administration! Let me rephrase the second paragraph of the above quote to reflect my personal observations.

> "On the other hand, the disinhibition effect may not be so benign. Out spills rude language, harsh criticisms, anger, hatred, even threats (the vast majority of which will be misspelled). Or people explore the dark underworld of the Internet, places of pornography and

> violence (eg. a typical chat room), places they would never visit in the real world (such as a mental health clinic). We might call this a 'typical behavior profile of the average cyber-kook.'"

But Dr. Suler does not limit himself to dry, overdone academic theories. In Chapter 6 he introduces us to a strange cyber-world known as "The Palace," which is best described as a cyber-gathering spot for those who had disassociated themselves from real-world, interpersonal communication and moved into a fantasy world that, while providing enough computer-generated illusions to at least present some semblance of a real place, was no more real than Winnie The Pooh's Hundred Acre Wood. (Note to the reader: The distant, wailing sound that you are hearing is not an indication that the malfunction of a three-dollar fan is about to destroy your fifteen hundred-dollar computer. It is merely the cries of anguish arising from the multitude of people who are heartbroken to learn that Owl and Piglet are also imaginary).

The Palace was one of the earliest (and yet still exemplary) multi-user chat rooms, although any attempt at a description of it would be hopelessly inadequate. It was an imaginary place (remember the Hundred Acre Wood analogy) that was programmed to resemble, well, a palace. (It seems originality with names, like emotional stability, is not a prerequisite in cyber-space). Within its imaginary walls one could find bars, reading rooms, studies, game rooms or just about anything else you could imagine. When it was launched in 1996 it represented the "cutting edge" of technology and was touted as the birth of yet another "revolutionary" facet of cyberspace.

The Palace, Dr. Suler informs us, was chosen because it was the opportunity to observe the "development" of a cyber-society complete with social norms, authority figures and every other trapping of a real-world social system. Naturally, it failed to do so. Suler advances several factors that led to the Palace's transformation from the capitol of the cyber-promised land into the electronic equivalent of a Bombay slum.

He first notes what may appear to be proof that the "cyber-world" often mimics real world dynamics by pointing out the social pressures that resulted from a rapidly expanding population of newcomers during the first year of the Palace's existence. The original "inhabitants" of the Palace tended to be relatively well educated, responsible adults who were genuinely interested in forming what might be described as an on-line social club. The majority of these newcomers, however, had the social graces of the barbarian hordes that over ran the Roman Empire coupled with pre-existing psychosocial pathologies that made them unstable in the real world, much less in cyber-space. The results were essentially the same. The Palace promptly degenerated into anarchy since the barbarians outnumbered the civilized settlers, even on a good day, by a factor of approximately two hundred to one. Dr. Suler offers the following explanation of the dynamics involved.

> "In any growing population—be it virtual or 'real'—people struggle to find their place among the masses. People want to feel that they belong to a distinct group, and they also want their unique identity recognized within that group. They want to feel that they are contributing to the community—making their 'mark' on it. Within the mix of sundry people, they want to acquire some measure of status, position, and power—especially if they've been around a while. They want these things not necessarily to control or dominate others, but rather to feel a sense of personal value and importance. They want to be somebody, and not just anybody."

While these finding may have surprised Dr. Suler, any regular user of the Internet, be they chat room denizen or not, could have told him exactly the same thing: that if an individual is a psychiatric basket case in reality this same individual will also be a psychiatric basket case in cyber-space! To the best of this reviewer's knowledge there are no reported cases of a journey into cyber-space that has resulted in a Lourdes-like miraculous repair of what is usually a combination of faulty genetics, lousy interpersonal skills, and estrangement from even the lower boundaries of civil behavior. Nor has there been any indication that the "computer age," "information super-highway," "global village" or any other metaphor you might wish to use has had the slightest beneficial effect on the human race at all!

The Psychology of Cyberspace is notable in that it is the first popularly-available study of this new realm of human experience. In defense of Dr. Suler, I will be the first to point out that he is indeed a pioneer in that 1) cyberspace is indeed *terra incognito* at best and is probably closer to *terra infirma* if we wish to stay with the impressive but not very descriptive Latin and also that 2) it is going to be harder than Hell to find anything with which to compare his results. This is indeed unfortunate because I personally would like to see anything as chaotic as cyberspace subjected to even an attempt at scientific analysis.

In fact, I would also be interested in seeing the sun rise in the west, since this is infinitely more likely to occur than the publication of a full explanation of human behavior in that dismal cyber-swamp into which Dr. Suler has dipped his academic toes.

Bibliography

Suler, J. *The Psychology of Cyberspace*. (November, 2004 edition). Available electronically at www.rider.edu/suler/psycyber/psycyber.html

11.

Sex in Wonderland

No matter where you go, there you are.

Yogi Berra

I put off completing this section for as long as I could, but I ran out of things to write about. So get ready for the climactic (no pun intended) act of the Theater Of The Absurd known as "chat," a visit to the intellectual swamp known as the "Adult Chat Rooms."

Since the "adult" areas obey the basic laws of the other rooms, your chances of finding anyone with even close to an adult mentality in adult chat are even lower than encountering a sapient life form anywhere else in the chat universe. But, when you add a title to something you have somehow legitimized it. The same is true with "adult chat", which is a misleading name for an area where inflated egos and sick minds can gather without having to worry about whether anyone is actually believing the pack of lies about being a "6'2" 215 pound blond fireman" from someone who is, in reality, a pimple-faced 19 year-old that makes Pee Wee Herman look like Luke Perry and hyperventilates while looking at the Sears and Roebuck catalog.

The "adult" rooms are the ninth, and lowest, circle of the infernal pits known as chat rooms and are a place where schizophrenia may be considered a social asset. Needless to say such rooms are populated with people that you don't even want to meet in cyberspace, much less in real life. This fact is not lost on the denizens of this area, who have taken considerable liberties when it comes to presenting complimentary and somewhat enhanced physical descriptions of themselves while simultaneously lying between their two remaining teeth. Every woman in an adult chat room is a twenty three-year-old blond college cheerleader who is lonely and looking for a handsome young male model to fulfill here wildest sexual fantasies. There is never a shortage of such virile young men, because all males in the adult rooms have acquired the unusual ability to change their physical appearances to conform to the desires of any female that they may encounter.

The Lay (No Pun Intended, Again) Of the Land

Before you gain admission to this sexual Disney World you are confronted with the usual disclaimers and warnings about who is eligible for entry into this Never-Never Land. This "small print" is, of course, designed to protect the people who actually own the servers and routers that make up the physical components of a chat room from lawsuits and legal charges relating to providing obscene materials to minors via the Internet.

Your first encounter with the world of "Adult" chat is generally of the form:

WARNING!

You are attempting to enter an area devoted, but not limited to, discussions devoted to explicit sexual matter. By entering this area, you certify that you are an adult over the age of eighteen and that you acknowledge the presence of such explicit subject matter and agree not to hold the operators of this site responsible for any consequences resulting from exposure to such matter.

Since this notice contains too many words not in the vocabulary of most chatters, and since most underage chatters have difficulty reading beyond the "See Spot Run" level, the above notice might as well say:

CONGRATULATIONS!

You managed to find the weirdo rooms! Since we don't really care how old you are, click the "Enter Adult Chat" button and come on in. Just remember, if mommy and daddy catch you jerking off don't start crying about how you didn't know what you were getting into. You should have either learned to read or developed enough social skills to at least have a realistic chance of getting laid.

Once you are past this formidable obstacle, you are presented with a menu of rooms devoted to such things as:

1. *BD/SM:* supposedly "bondage and/or discipline" and "sadism and/or masochism" but could be devoted to "brain dead spanking the monkey."

2. *Fetishes:* feet, ankles, knees, panty hose, high heels, rubber suits, getting gang-raped by Hottentot tribesmen wearing Ross Perot Halloween masks (and I only made it from the feet to waist-level. Use your imagination as to what else falls in the shade of this umbrella).

3. *Gay Male:* Brad sneaks away from Buffy to meet Bruce.

4. *Lesbian:* self-explanatory, although given the sorry state of most male chatters, this could be a very crowded room.

5. *Married but Looking:* Ma and Pa Kettle on the loose in cyberspace.

6. *Masturbation:* fortunately, also self-explanatory because Mark Twain and Charles Dickens together couldn't write an explanation that would do justice to this room.

7. *Role Playing:* devoted to the standard chat room practice of lying, but in a more romantic, fantasy setting.

8. *Straight:* for those with limited imaginations or who have yet to decide on a favored form of recreational sex.

This is not a complete roster, of course, of the rooms available to the sexually-oriented chat room user. To provide a complete listing would tax both the ability of this writer to objectively report his findings as well as the sufficiency of the English language to provide the words to accurately describe them, without being forced to develop an entirely new dialect.

What I can do is provide a very basic overview of the demographics of those frequenting of this corner of the chat world, which might also convince you to avoid this area at all costs.

The male to female ratio in the adult chat area is about 63:1, with median ages being 22 for males and 35 for females. Why these ages seem to predominate is totally beyond comprehension unless these ages represent what I refer to as the "Ages of Absolutely No Concept of Reality." This may be due to the fact that males at this particular age seem to feel that they are nothing less than every woman's fantasy and cannot understand why the few females in adult chat are not groveling at their feet begging for recognition.

The female chatter in this area tends to be somewhat insecure as to her own self-image and desirability, usually because they have finally realized that they are pushing forty and Prince Charming still hasn't shown up to save them from a life with Bubba Joe Junior and a rented mobile home filled with a herd of screaming hyperactive children from their combined five previous marriages.

Another interesting observation about the so-called adult chatters is their geographic distribution. Practically all the females in the adult chat rooms are from the United States, England or Canada (with a smattering from other Western Hemisphere locations). This is definitely not the case with the males, of which at least fifty per cent seem to come from Obscuristan, Gallup, New Mexico or some other God-forsaken Third World cesspool.

If you should wander into the adult chat rooms with anything resembling a feminine-sounding screen name, be ready for a barrage of private messages that basically follow the same format. The following is an actual exchange of messages I received while using the name "Audens_tears."

Idiot: HAI! a/s/l please
Me: Go away

(About a one minute pause, then)

Idiot: a/s/l

Me: old male, now go away

(Another pause)

Idiot: You will talk to me

Me: NO!! GO AWAY!!!!!

(Another one minute pause)

Idiot: a/s/l

I then responded with a string of profanity that would have embarrassed a Marine Corps Sergeant Major, which I will not reproduce here on the outside chance my mother might read this. Did that get the point across to this moron? Of course not!

Idiot: Why you not will talk to me?

Me: Because I f______g don't want to!

(Another pause)

Idiot: a/s/l please

Me: You get the iggy moron

As I mentioned earlier, the adult chat rooms are roughly divided into sections based on the particular flavor of deviancy being practiced. Fortunately, we don't have to visit each room individually to get an impression of what actually goes on.

The first thing to remember is that, like any other category of chat, truth is on an extended leave of absence in the adult rooms. Things like the Biblical admonitions regarding bestiality and common sense seem to be missing as well, particularly if you encounter a chatter that has such an inflated ego that it leads them to use a web cam.

Having a web cam is a guarantee that you will attract all the attention you could possibly want. If getting bombarded with Instant Messages from semi-literate teen aged morons or from oversexed semi-literate Third World morons is your idea of a fun night in chat, you will think that you have died and gone to Chat Room Heaven. And, if you have a screen name that might be taken as feminine AND a web cam, you will spend the rest of the night/day/weekend/your life getting hammered by messages from these clowns.

Inside The Mind (And Other Empty Places) Of the "Adult" Chatter

Compared to other parts of the cyber-universe, the adult chat rooms are, for the most part, actually quite tame with "tame," being defined as in relation to mass hysteria. In other words, what is considered "tame" in cyber-space is usually sufficient to get you involuntarily committed for a psychiatric evaluation in most civilized countries or beheaded in some "Islamic Republics."

I consider adult chat as "tame" because the participants are, as a rule, rendered harmless by the simple fact that there isn't a snowball's chance in Hell you would want to personally meet anyone that you might encounter online. This single observation can be taken to its next level to prove that, as long as you avoid anyone that you have first encountered online, your chances of becoming a statistic at the FBI's Psychological Profiling Unit approaches your chances of winning the lottery.

As in other chat rooms there is something of a social hierarchy in the adult rooms, but one's position in that hierarchy is self-assigned and is determined by multiplying one's degree of self-importance by the number of diagnosed social pathologies present. Naturally, this means that everyone assumes themselves to be everyone else's idea of perfection which in turn sets the stage for the inevitable showdown known, in chat room slang, as "drama."

Before continuing, a brief review of online psychology.

As noted in a previous chapter John Suler, PhD. has identified what he calls the "online disinhibition effect" which can be loosely summarized as "anonymity + computer = asshole." This "effect" is encountered so frequently in the adult chat rooms that eventually you become so acclimated to idiotic behavior that such behavior appears "more normal than 'normal.'"

"Drama" is a direct consequence of Suler's disinhibition effect and usually begins when friction between two inflated egos reaches ignition temperature and the combatants, cheered on by their respective followers, trade insults until they reach the PMA (point of maximum absurdity) and the room dialog begins to resemble the "Taunting" scene in *Monty Python and the Holy Grail*:

> *French Knight:* I don't want to talk to you no more, you empty headed animal food trough water! I fart in your general direction! You mother was a hamster and your father smelt of elderberries!
>
> *Lancelot:* Is there someone else up there we could talk to?
>
> *French Knight:* No, now go away or I shall taunt you a second time!

The eternal saga of "adult" chat is also the subject of several web-based commentators such as Regina Lynn, who writes on the wired.com web site. Regina Lynn's columns are noteworthy in that they are, for all practical purposes, the only rational commentary on the subjects of "cyber-sex," online pornography and, thanks to our Christian chat room friends, censorship.

As an example, in January 2005 she opened a dialog with her readers with a column entitled "Desperately Seeking Cyber-sex" which examined the contention by some that "Internet porn addiction" and "Cyber-sex addiction" are threatening the stability of the Western hemisphere.

Lest you think that I have misrepresented the subject, check this out:

> "I looked, this past week, for good cyber…it was hard to find a chat room where people were indeed chatting, much less flirting or attempting intelligent seduction.

> Instead it was "any white chikc want 2 talk to eas India guy?" and "hunny r u wearing ur bikini?" Not exactly riveting."
>
> (www.wired.com/news/culture/0,1284,66344,00.html)

I agree with her opinion. If tolerating nonsense such as that is addictive then we, as a species, are doomed.

Her follow-up column contained what I feel is one of the better explanation of the ongoing evolution of cyberspace in general and chat rooms in particular.

> "Many blame the deterioration of sex chat on the influx of AOL members exploring IRC for the first time, thanks to the newfangled web-based user interfaces. It was "pretty much the universal death knell of some of the big [chat] hangouts, as if a half-thousand Paris Hiltons suddenly showed up to the best party ever…"
>
> (www.wired.com/news/culture/0,1284,66423,00.html)

Once again I agree. When we began to teach children how to use a PC, the influx of childish adults couldn't have been too far behind.

It Takes a Child to Raze a Village

Lest you think the upcoming generation will learn from our mistakes, I call your attention to the following transcript which was sent to me by a friend that wanted to prove to me that I was being entirely too kind when I referred to one chat room clown that was whining about being 'underage' relative to the drinking laws as a "lobotomized goat." I am not making this up. (See this web site, which is sponsored by Planned Parenthood, http://www.teenwire.com/ask/articles/as_20010517p221.asp)

Ask the Experts!

Dear Experts:

What is cyber-sex? I was online and someone asked me if I wanted to 'cyber' What happens during cyber-sex?

Shidia

I will not publish the reply to this question due to my desire to avoid a copyright problem, but I did give you the URL that this example comes from. Spend a few minutes reading some of the things posted there and then try to convince yourself that mandatory birth control and/or sterilization is a bad idea.

Among the other mysteries of life discussed on this particular web site are these questions posed by the products of our superior American education system:

Can I get chlamydia in my mouth?

I love my boyfriend but the other day he hit my face. What should I do?

Can I get pregnant from making out in the swimming pool?

My boyfriend has genital warts. Can I get it from him by kissing or having oral sex?

These questions are not totally inane because they do make one very important point that both sides (the "just say no" versus the "anything goes" mobs) of the sex education debate should readily concede: If all the money and controversy about sex education in the public school systems over the past twenty years has brought us to this level of awareness, it is time to stop wasting the taxpayer's money!

***

We have now reached the end of our little joyride down the Information Superhighway. Our once-shiny convertible is now covered in mud, its tires bald, and its windshield cracked in at least a dozen places. The radiator is overheating and the bumper is dented from repeated collisions with stupidity.

But, we have persevered because our hearts are pure and our courage knows no bounds.

And if you believe that load of bullshit, you belong in a chat room.

12.

Friends: In All the Right Places

If you have read the other chapters of this book or are one of my regular on-line readers, you know by now that I have very little respect for most of the people that I encounter in "real life," much less the denizens of the Internet. And now, just to keep you on your toes, rather than an essay dealing with the previous chapter I'm going to share with you a lesson that I learned one night in, of all places, an Internet chat room. A lesson in what friendship can mean in a world called cyber-space.

Friendship is among the most fickle of things, regardless of where you might find yourself. When you think it's there, it isn't. Let the sun shine and you have friends all around you. But let it rain, and you can't borrow a newspaper to make a poor man's umbrella. When fortune smiles on you, others want to be nearby in the hopes that some of that fortune will perhaps follow them. Let your fortunes reverse and you can't pay those same people to look you in the eye. And now I'm going to do something I don't do very often, or maybe I don't do often enough: I'm going to admit that I was wrong about something. Very, very wrong indeed.

I had always thought that, being an observer of the human condition, I could usually predict the response of the crowds to a given situation. I thought that the basic response of us humans was the same as elsewhere in the animal kingdom, which was to turn our backs to one who was in pain, or feeling a loss that was tearing into all that they had ever trusted or believed in. Or, if I dare use that word, had faith in.

In the cyber-world, you never physically meet someone. You let your mind's eye give them a face but you never see that face. You never learn if you were right about how you imagined that they look, or talk. And I never dreamed that I would see people who never met, and probably never will meet, come together to comfort some anonymous person that, like themselves, lives as a few lines of type on a screen. But I saw it. And I felt it too.

A friend, a real friend, was hurting. And every person there felt it. And every one of them seemed to be making a silent wish that they could somehow bend the laws of time and space itself to reach out, to hold, to comfort someone they know only by a name. Don't ask me to explain how that happened. I've always worshiped in the temple of science but my science can't explain things like empathy, compassion, or love. But there were these people, themselves only names, responding as if it were a neighbor or even a family member of theirs. And I felt, for the first time in a long, long while, that these people actually cared about someone, feeling another's pain and confusion. And I knew that each one would have gladly done anything to ease that pain. They were responding not because some social convention that said it was the proper thing to do but because a part of them wanted to do it. That part of them was something else that I can't measure, or even understand, with the tools of science. It came from their souls. I like to think that, on that night, I saw souls reaching out to comfort another soul. That's the only way I can think of to explain it.

And deep inside me I hope that is indeed what I saw. I hope I saw whatever it is that makes us human reacting in the way we humans should react when a fellow member of this blundering herd is in pain. Because if I did, there could yet be hope for us all.

Printed in the United States
45612LVS00002B/37-42

9 781413 789942